Nuns & the Great War
1914-18

Nuns & the Great War 1914-18

The Irish Nuns at Ypres

D. M. C.

From Convent to Conflict
or
A Nun's Account of the Invasion of Belgium

Sister M Antonia

LEONAUR

Nuns & the Great War 1914-18
The Irish Nuns at Ypres
by D. M. C.
From Convent to Conflict
or
A Nun's Account of the Invasion of Belgium
by Sister M Antonia

FIRST EDITION

First published under the titles
The Irish Nuns at Ypres
and
From Convent to Conflict
Or
A Nun's Account of the Invasion of Belgium

Leonaur is an imprint
of Oakpast Ltd

ISBN: 978-1-78282-377-3 (hardcover)
ISBN: 978-1-78282-378-0 (softcover)

http://www.leonaur.com

Contents

The Irish Nuns at Ypres

The Mother Prioress of Ypres

The Lady Abbess at Oulton. The Lady Abess of Ypres
OULTON AND YPRES

Contents

Preface

The following narrative was originally intended, as a record of the events it relates, for the use of the community only. But, shortly after the arrival of the Mother Prioress in England, the manuscript was placed in my hands. I soon formed the opinion that it deserved a larger circulation. My friend Reginald Smith shared this view, and so the story has come before the public. It is in truth a human document of thrilling interest, and will, I believe, make an abiding contribution to the history of this worldwide war. D. M. C, though a novice in literary work, describes with graphic force the transactions in which she and her sisters played so conspicuous and so courageous a part. The moving pictures, which pass before our eyes in her pages, are full of touching realism, and throw curious side-lights on the manifold aspects of the titanic struggle which comes home to everyone and everything.

The heroism, the self-devotion, the religious faith, the Christian zeal and charity of those Irish nuns at Ypres, in a terrible crisis in the history of their Order, will, I venture to say, command universal respect and admiration, mingled with pity for their fate, and an earnest desire, among all generous souls, to help them in retrieving their fortunes.

A note by the prioress, and an introduction by Mr. Redmond, who, amid his many onerous occupations, is not unmindful of the duty which Irishmen owe to the historic little community of Irish Nuns at Ypres, form a foreword to a narrative which belongs to the history of the times.

On the subject of one of the flags captured by the Irish Brigade at the Battle of Ramillies, (still preserved in the convent 1915), I have added a note in the text at the end of chapter 3.

There are names in Belgium which revive memories that Irishmen cannot forget. Fontenoy and Landen are household words. Ypres, too, brings back recollections associated with deeds which mark the devotion of the Irish people to Faith and Fatherland.

R. Barry O'Brien.

100 Sinclair Road,
Kensington, W. May 1915.

Note by Prioress

These simple notes, destined at first for the intimacy of our abbey, we now publish through the intervention of Mr. Barry O'Brien to satisfy the numerous demands of friends, who, owing to the horrors of the fighting round Ypres, have shown great interest in our welfare.

Owing, also, to the numerous articles about us, appearing daily in the newspapers—and which, to say the least, are often very exaggerated—I have charged Dame M. Columban to give a detailed account of all that has befallen the community, since the coming of the Germans to Ypres till our safe arrival at Oulton Abbey. I can therefore certify that all that is in this little book, taken from the notes which several of the nuns had kept, is perfectly true, and only a simple narrative of our own personal experiences of the war.

May this account, to which Mr. Redmond has done us the honour of writing an introduction at the request of Dame Teresa, his niece, bring us some little help towards the rebuilding of our beloved and historic monastery, which, this very year, (1915), should celebrate its 250th anniversary.

M. Maura, O.S.B.,
Prioress. April 1915.

Introduction

I have been asked to write an introduction to this book, but I feel that I can add little to its intense dramatic interest.

Ypres has been one of the chief centres of the terrible struggle which is now proceeding on the Continent, and it is well known that this same old Flemish town has figured again and again in the bloody contests of the past.

It may, perhaps, be well to explain, in a few words, how the tide of war has once more rolled to this old-world city.

On Sunday, June 28, 1914, in Sarajevo, the capital of Bosnia, the Archduke Francis Ferdinand of Austria-Hungary and his wife, the Duchess of Hohenberg, were assassinated. Although it was known throughout Europe that there was in existence in Serbia an anti-Austrian conspiracy (not of a very formidable character), and although suspicion pointed towards the assassinations being due in some way to the influence of this conspiracy, no one dreamt for a moment that the tragedy which had occurred would have serious European consequences; and, as a matter of fact, it was not until July 23 that the Austro-Hungarian Government presented an ultimatum to Serbia.

On that day, however, a note of a most extraordinary and menacing character was delivered to the Serbian Government by Austria-Hungary. It contained no less than ten separate demands, including the suppression of newspapers and literature; the disappearance of all nationalist societies; the reorganisation of Government schools; wholesale dismissal of officers from the army; and an extraordinary demand that Austro-Hungarian officials should have a share in all judicial proceedings in Serbia; besides the arrest of certain specified men, and the prevention of all traffic in arms.

It at once became evident to the whole world that no nation could possibly agree to these demands and maintain a semblance of national independence; and, when it was found that the ultimatum required a reply within forty-eight hours, it became clear that the whole of Europe was on the brink of a volcano.

Great Britain, through Sir Edward Grey, had already urged Serbia to show moderation and conciliation in her attitude towards Austria-Hungary; and, when the ultimatum was submitted to her. Great Britain and Russia both urged upon her the necessity of a moderate and conciliatory answer.

As a matter of fact, Serbia agreed to every one of the demands in the Austro-Hungarian ultimatum, with only two reservations, and on these she proposed to submit the questions in dispute to The Hague. Serbia received no reply from Austria-Hungary; and, immediately on the expiration of the forty-eight hours, the Austro-Hungarian Minister quitted Belgrade. During those forty-eight hours. Great Britain and Russia had urged (1) that the time-limit for the ultimatum should be extended, and that Germany should join in this demand; but Germany refused. Sir Edward Grey then proposed (2) that Great Britain, France, Germany, and Italy should act together, both in Austria-Hungary and in Russia, in favour of peace. Italy agreed; France agreed; Russia agreed; but Germany again held back. Sir Edward Grey then proposed (3) that the German, Italian, and French Ambassadors should meet him in London. Italy and France agreed; Russia raised no objection; but Germany refused.

On July 29, the German Imperial Chancellor made to the British Ambassador in Berlin the extraordinary and historic proposal that Great Britain should remain neutral, provided that Germany undertook not to invade Holland, and to content herself with seizing the colonies of France, and further promised that, if Belgium remained passive and allowed German troops to violate her neutrality by marching through Belgium into France, no territory would be taken from her. The only possible answer was returned by Great Britain in the rejection of what Mr. Asquith called 'an infamous proposal.'

On July 31, the British Government demanded from the German and French Governments an undertaking, in accordance with treaty obligations, to respect Belgium's neutrality, and demanded from the Belgian Government an undertaking to uphold it. France at once gave the necessary undertaking, as did Belgium. Germany made no reply whatever, and from that moment war was inevitable.

On Monday, August 3, the solemn treaty, guaranteeing the neutrality of Belgium, signed by Germany as well as by France and Great

Britain, was treated as 'a scrap of paper,' to be thrown into the waste-paper basket by Germany; Belgian territory was invaded by German troops; and, on the next day, Tuesday, August 4, German troops attacked Liege. From August 4 to August 15, Liege, under its heroic commander. General Leman, barred the advance of the German armies, and, in all human probability, saved Paris and France and the liberties of Europe.

On August 17, the Belgian Government withdrew from Brussels to Antwerp. On August 20, Brussels was occupied by the Germans. On August 24, Namur was stormed. On August 25, Louvain was destroyed, and, after weeks of bloody warfare, after the retreat from Mons to the Marne, and the victorious counter-attack which drove the Germans back across the Aisne and to their present line of defence, Antwerp was occupied by the Germans on the 9th of October. On October 11, what may be called the battle of Ypres began in real earnest; but the town, defended by the Allies, held heroically out; and by November 20, the utter failure of the attempt of the Germans to break through towards Calais by the Ypres route was acknowledged by everyone.

During the interval, Ypres was probably the centre of the most terrible fighting in the War. This delightful old Flemish town, with its magnificent cathedral and its unique Cloth Hall, probably the finest specimen of Gothic architecture in Europe, was wantonly bombarded day and night. The Germans have failed to capture the old city; but they have laid it in ruins.

The following pages show the sufferings and heroism of the present members of a little community of Irish nuns, which '*The world forgetting, by the world forgot,*' has existed in Ypres since the days, some two hundred and fifty years ago, when their Royal Abbey was first established. It is true that, during those centuries, Ypres has more than once been subjected to bombardment and attack, and, more than once, *Les Dames Irlandaises* of the Royal Benedictine Abbey of Ypres have been subjected to suffering and danger. But never before were they driven from their home and shelter.

Why, it may be asked, is there a little community of Irish Benedictine nuns at Ypres? During the reign of Queen Elizabeth, three English ladies—Lady Percy, with Lady Montague, Lady Fortescue and others—wishing to become Religious, and being unable to do so in their own country, assembled at Brussels and founded an English House of the ancient Order of St. Benedict. Their numbers increasing, they made affiliations at Ghent, Dunkerque, and Pontoise.

In the year 1665, the Vicar-General of Ghent was made the Bishop of Ypres, and he founded there a Benedictine Abbey, with the Lady Marina Beaumont as its first Lady Abbess. In the year 1682, on the death of the first Lady Abbess, Lady Flavia Cary was chosen as the first Irish Lady Abbess of what was intended to be at that date, and what has remained down to the present day, an Irish community. At that time, the Irish had no other place for Religious in Flanders. A legal donation and concession of the house of Ypres was made in favour of the Irish nation, and was dedicated to the Immaculate Conception under the title of 'Gratia Dei.' Irish nuns from other houses were sent to Ypres to form the first Irish community. From that day to this, there have been only two Lady Abbesses of Ypres who have not been Irish, and the community has always been, so far as the vast majority of its members are concerned, composed of Irish ladies.

Its history,[1] which has been published, contains the names of the various Lady Abbesses. They are, practically, all Irish, with the familiar names Butler, O'Bryan, Ryan, Mandeville, Dalton, Lynch, and so on.

In 1687, James II of England desired the Lady Abbess of the day, Lady Joseph Butler, to come over from Ypres to Dublin and to found an Abbey there under the denomination of 'His Majesty's Chief Royal Abbey.' In 1688, the Lady Abbess, accompanied by some others of the community at Ypres, arrived in Dublin, and established the Abbey in Big Ship Street, leaving the House at Ypres in the charge of other members of the community. It is recorded that, when passing through London, she was received by the queen, at Whitehall, in the habit of her Order, which had not been seen there since the Reformation. In Dublin, James II received her, and granted her a Royal Patent, giving the community 'house, rent, postage' free, and an annuity of £100. This Royal Patent, with the Great Seal of the Kingdom, was in the custody of the nuns at Ypres when this war began. It was dated June 5, 1689.

When William III arrived in Dublin, in 1690, he gave permission to the Lady Abbess, Lady Butler, to remain. But she and her nuns refused, saying ' they would not live under a usurper.' William then gave her a pass to Flanders, and this particular letter was also amongst the treasures at Ypres when the war broke out.

Notwithstanding William's free pass, the Irish Abbey in Dublin was broken into and pillaged by the soldiery, and it was with difficulty that

---

1. *The Irish Dames of Ypres,* by the Rev. Dom Patrick Nolan, O.S.B.

the Sisters and the Lady Abbess made their way, after long and perilous journeys, home to their House at Ypres. They brought with them many relics from Dublin, including some old oak furniture, which was used in the abbey at Ypres up to the recent flight of the community.

And so the Irish Abbey at Ypres has held its ground, with varying fortunes. In January, 1793, forty or fifty armed soldiers broke into the abbey; but the Lady Abbess of the day went to Tournai to seek aid from the general-in-chief, who was an Irishman. He withdrew the troops from the Convent. The following year, however, Ypres was besieged by the French; but, although the city was damaged, the Convent, almost miraculously, escaped without injury.

An order for the suppression of convents was issued in the very height of the Revolution. The heroic Lady Abbess Lynch died. She was succeeded by her sister. Dame Bernard Lynch, and the community were ordered to leave. They were, however, prevented from so doing by a violent storm which broke over the town, and next day there was a change of government, and the Irish Dames and the Irish Abbey were allowed to remain, and, for several years the Irish Abbey was the only convent of any Order existing in the Low Countries.[2]

So it has remained on to the present day, from the year 1682 down to 1915, when, for the first time during that long period, this little Irish community has been driven from Ypres and its convent laid in ruins.

Amongst the other relics and antiquities treasured by the community at Ypres, at the opening of this war, was the famous flag, so often spoken of in song and story, captured by the Irish Brigade in the service of France at the Battle of Ramillies; a voluminous correspondence with James II; a large border of lace worked by Mary Stuart; a large painted portrait of James II, presented by him to the abbey; a church vestment made of gold horse-trappings of James II; another vestment made from the dress of the Duchess Isabella, representing the King of Spain in the Netherlands; and a number of other most valuable relics of the past.

All these particulars can be verified by reference to the Rev. Dom Patrick Nolan's valuable history.

This little community is now in exile in England. Their abbey and

---

2. At the time of the Revolution, the nuns of Brussels and Dunkerque (to which Pontoise had been united) and Ghent fled to England, and these three Houses are now represented by Bergholt Abbey (Brussels), Teignmouth (Dunkerque), and Oulton Abbey (Ghent).

beautiful church are in ruins. Some of their precious relics are believed to be in places of safety. But most of their property has been destroyed. They escaped, it is true, with their lives. But what is their future to be? Surely Irishmen, to whom the subject especially appeals, and English sympathisers who appreciate courage and fortitude, will sincerely desire to help those devoted and heroic nuns to go back to Ypres—the home of the community for over two centuries—to rebuild their abbey and reopen their schools, to continue in their honourable mission of charity and benevolence, and to resume that work of education in which their Order has been so long and so successfully engaged.

John E. Redmond.

April 1915.

CHAPTER 1

The Coming of the Germans

The war, with all its horrors, into which the Emperor of Germany plunged the world in August 1914, had been raging nearly six weeks, when, towards the end of September, vague rumours of the enemy's approach reached us at Ypres. Several villages in the neighbourhood had had visits from the dreaded *Uhlans*, and, according to report, more than one prisoner had avowed that they were on their way to Ypres. An aeroplane had even been sent from Ghent to survey the town, but had lost its way. In these circumstances, the burgomaster sent round word that from henceforward, until further orders, no strong lights should be seen from the outside, and no bells should be rung from six in the evening till the following day. Consequently, when night came on, the monastery remained in darkness, each nun contenting herself with the minimum of light; and a few strokes of a little hand-bell summoned the community to hours of regular observance, instead of the well-known sound of the belfry-bell, which had, for so many years, fearlessly made known each succeeding hour.

Another result of the *burgomaster's* notice was that we were no longer able to say the office in the choir, as on one side the windows looked on the street, and on the other to the garden, the light being thus clearly visible from the ramparts. We, therefore, said *compline* and *matins*, first in the work-room, and afterwards in the chapter-house, placing a double set of curtains on the windows to prevent the least little glimmer of light from being seen from the outside.

An uneasy feeling of uncertainty took possession of the town. This feeling increased as news reached us, in the first days of October, that the enemy had been seen several times in the neighbourhood. At length, on October 7—a never-to-be-forgotten day for all those then at Ypres—a German aeroplane passed over the town, and shortly afterwards, at about 1.30 p.m., everyone was startled by the sound of firing at no great distance. In the monastery, it was the spiritual-reading hour, so we were not able to communicate our fears; but, instead of receding, the sound came nearer, till, at 2 o'clock, the shots from the guns literally made the house shake. Unable to surmise the cause of this sudden invasion, we went our way, trying to reassure ourselves as best we could. Shortly after vespers the sound of the little bell called us all together, and Reverend Mother Prioress announced to us, to our great dismay, that what we had feared had now taken place—the Germans were in the town.

Some poor persons, who came daily to the abbey to receive soup, had hastened to bring the dreadful tidings on hearing the bell ring for vespers, because an order had been issued (of which we were totally ignorant) that no bells might be rung, for fear of exciting suspicion. The poor, often more unselfish and kind-hearted than the rich, showed themselves truly so on this occasion, being more anxious for our safety than their own—one poor woman offering her little house as a shelter for Lady Abbess. She had only one penny for all her fortune, but still she was sure that everything would be well all the same; for, as she wisely remarked, the Germans were less likely to think of pillaging her bare rooms than our splendid monastery.

The cannonading which we had heard at 1.30 was a gallant defence made by 100 Belgian police, who had been obliged to retreat before the 15,000 Germans, who, from 2 till 8 p.m., poured slowly into the affrighted town, chanting a lugubrious war-song. M. Colaert, the *burgomaster*, and the principal men were obliged to present themselves. It was arranged that the town would be spared on the payment of 75,000 *francs*, and on condition that no further violence should be offered. M. Colaert and another gentleman were kept as hostages.

We looked at one another in consternation. We might then, at any moment, expect a visit, and what a visit! What if they were to come to ask lodgings for the night? We dared not refuse them. What if they ransacked the house? . . . Would they touch our beloved Lady Abbess, who, owing to a stroke she had had two years before, remained now partially paralysed? . . . We instinctively turned our steps to the choir. There, Mother Prioress began the rosary and, with all the fervour of our souls, an ardent cry mounted to the throne of the Mother of Mercy, 'Pray for us now, and at the hour of our death.' Was that hour about to strike? . . . After the rosary, we recommended ourselves to the endless bounty of the Sacred Heart, the Protector of our monastery, '*Coeur Sacré de Jésus, j'ai confiance en Vous.*' And putting all our confidence in the double protection of our Divine Spouse and His Immaculate Mother, we awaited the issue of events.

Our old servant-man Edmund—an honest, a fearless, and a reliable retainer, with certainly a comical side to his character—soon came in with news. Prompted by a natural curiosity, he had gone out late in the afternoon to see the troops; for the Germans, as in so many other towns, made an immense parade on entering Ypres. For six long hours they defiled in perfect order before the gazing multitude, who, although terrified, could not repress their desire to see such an unwonted spectacle. Following the army came huge guns, and cars of ammunition and provisions without end. The troops proceeded to the post office, where they demanded money from the safes. The Belgian officials stated that, owing to the troubled times, no great sum was kept there, and produced 200 *francs* (the rest having been previously hidden).

The railway station had also to suffer, the telegraph and telephone wires being all cut; while four German soldiers, posted at the corners of the public square, and relieved at regular intervals, armed with loaded revolvers, struck terror into the unfortunate inhabitants of Ypres. After some time, however, the most courageous ventured to open conversation with the invaders—amongst the others Edmund, who, coming across a soldier, more affable-looking than the rest, accosted him. The German, only too glad to seize the opportunity, replied civilly enough, and the two were soon in full conversation.

'You seem to be in great numbers here.'

'Oh! this is nothing compared to the rest! Germany is still full—we have millions waiting to come! We are sure to win, the French are only cowards!'

'Where are you going to when you leave Ypres?'

'To Calais!'

'And then?'

'To London!'

'Ha-ha-ha! You won't get there as easy as you think, they'll never let you in!'

'We can always get there in our Zeppelins.' . . . With this the German turned on his heel and tramped off.

It was now time to think of finding lodgings for the night. A great number of horses were put in the waiting-rooms at the station, destroying all the cushions and furniture. The soldiers demanded shelter

23

in whatever house they pleased, and no one dared refuse them any-thing. Our abbey, thanks to Divine Providence, of whose favour we were to receive so many evident proofs during the next two months, was spared from these unwelcome visitors—not one approached the house, and we had nothing to complain of but the want of bread. Our baker, being on the way to the convent with the loaves, was met by some German soldiers, who immediately laid hands on his cart, and emptied its contents. We therefore hastily made some soda-scones for supper, which, though not of the best, were nevertheless palatable. However, all did not escape so easily as we did, and many were the tales told of that dreadful night.

The most anxious of all were those who were actually housing wounded Belgian soldiers! If they were discovered, would the brave fellows not be killed there and then? And it happened, in more than one case, that they escaped by the merest chance. Before the convent of exiled French nuns, Rue de Lille, whom we were afterwards to meet at our stay at Poperinghe, and where at that moment numbers of Belgians were hidden, a German stopped a lady, who was luckily a great friend of the nuns, and asked if there were any wounded there. 'That is not a hospital,' she replied, 'but only a school'; and with a tone of assurance she added, 'If you do not believe me, you can go and see for yourself.'

The soldier answered, ' I believe you,' and passed on.

In another ease, the Germans entered a house where the Belgians were, and passed the night in the room just underneath them! A jew-eller's shop was broken into, and the property destroyed or stolen; and in a private dwelling, the lady of the house, finding herself alone with four officers—her husband having been taken as hostage—she took to flight, on which the Germans went all through the place, doing considerable damage. In other cases, they behaved pretty civilly. Our washerwoman had thirty to breakfast, of whom several had slept in her establishment, leading their horses into her drawing-room!

On seeing her little boys, they had exclaimed, 'Here are some brave little soldiers for us, later on!' And, on the mother venturing a mild expostulation, they added, 'Yes, you are all Germans now—Belgo-Germans'; while, before leaving, they wrote on her board—'We are Germans; we fear no one; we fear only God and our Emperor!' What troubled her the most was that her unwelcome guests had laid hold of her clean washing, taking all that they wanted; amongst other things, our towels had disappeared. We were, as may well be imagined, but too pleased to be rid of the dread Germans at so little cost.

It appears that while the German Army was still in Ypres, some 12,000 British soldiers, having followed on its track, stopped at a little distance from the town, sending word to the *burgomaster* that, if he wished, they were ready to attack the enemy. M. Colaert, however, not desiring to see the town given up to pillage and destruction, was opposed to a British advance.

By this time the whole town was on the *qui vive*, and no one thought of anything else but how best to secure any valuables that they had; for the stories of what had happened in other parts of Belgium were not at all reassuring. Several tried to leave the town; but the few trains that were running were kept exclusively for the troops, while the Germans sent back all those who left on foot. To increase the panic, no less than five aeroplanes passed during the day; and the knowledge that the enemy had left soldiers with two *mitrailleuses* at the Porte de Lille, to guard the town, completed the feeling of insecurity. Moreover—as the soldiers had literally emptied the town of all the eatables they could lay their hands on—sinister rumours of famine were soon spread abroad.

Reverend Mother Prioress sent out immediately for some sacks of flour, but none was to be got; and we were obliged to content ourselves with wheat-meal instead. Rice, coffee, and butter we had, together with some tins of fish. The potatoes were to come that very day, and great was our anxiety lest the cart would be met by the Germans and the contents seized. However, the farmer put off coming for some days, and at length arrived safely with the load, a boy going in front to see that no soldiers were about. The milk-woman, whose farm was a little way outside the town, was unable to come in, and no meat could be got for love or money; so we were obliged to make the best of what we had, and each day Mother Prioress went to the kitchen herself to see if she could not possibly make a new dish from the never varying meal—rice, Quaker oats, and *maizena*.

Ultimately the Allies came to our help, and a motorcar, armed with a *mitrailleuse*, flew through the streets and opened fire on the Germans. Taken by surprise, the latter ran to their guns; but, through some mishap, the naphtha took fire in one of them, whereupon the Germans retreated. Three of their men were wounded, and one civilian killed. On the Friday, we began to breathe freely again, when suddenly news came, even to the abbey, that one hundred Germans were parading round the town. On Sunday, the Allies came once more to chase them;

but, for the moment, the Germans had disappeared. Things continued thus for some days, until, to the delight of the inhabitants, the British took entire possession of the town, promising that the Germans would never enter it again. Just one week after the coming of the Germans, the troops of the Allies poured in, until, amid the enthusiastic cheers of the people, 21,000 soldiers filled the streets. Those who came by the monastery passed down the Rue St. Jacques singing lustily:

Here we are, here we are, here we are again:
Here we are, here we are, here we are again!

Then alternately each side repeated; 'Hallo! Hallo! Hallo! Hallo!' The crowd, whose knowledge of the English language did not extend far enough to enable them to grasp the meaning of 'Here we are again' soon, however, caught up the chorus of 'Hallo! Hallo!' and quickly the street resounded with cries, which were certainly discordant, but which, nevertheless, expressed the enthusiastic joy of the people.

CHAPTER 2

The Allies in Ypres

The contrast between the reception of the two armies was striking. On the arrival of the Germans, people kept in their houses, or looked at the foe with frightened curiosity; now, everyone lined the streets, eager for a glimpse of the brave soldiers who had come to defend Ypres. A week before, the citizens had furnished food to the enemy, because they dared not refuse it—and only then what they were obliged to give. Now, each one vied with the other in giving. Bread, butter, milk, chocolate—everything they had—went to the soldiers, and sounds of rejoicing came from all sides. Perhaps, the most pleased of all were the poor wounded Belgians, who had been so tried the preceding week. All those who were able to drag themselves along crowded to the windows and doors, to welcome their new comrades; and the latter, unable to make themselves understood by words, made vigorous signs that they were about to chop off the Germans' heads.

What excited the most curiosity were the 'petticoats,' as they were styled, of the Highlanders, and everyone gave their opinion on this truly extraordinary uniform, which had not been previously seen in these parts. The soldiers were quartered in the different houses and establishments of the town. Once more the abbey was left unmolested, though once again also the want of bread was felt—not, that it had been this time stolen, but that, in spite of all their efforts, the bakers could not supply the gigantic demand for bread necessary to feed our newly arrived friends. Seeing that we were likely to be forgotten in the general excitement, Edmund was sent out to see what he could find. After many vain efforts, he at last succeeded in getting three very small-sized loaves, with which he returned in triumph. Scarcely had he got inside the parlour, when there came a vigorous tug at the bell. The newcomer proved to be a man who, having caught sight of the

27

bread, came to beg some for 'his soldiers.'

Edmund was highly indignant, and loudly expostulated; but the poor man, with tears in his eyes, turned to Mother Prioress (who had just entered), and offered to pay for the bread, if only she would give him a little. 'I have my own son at the front,' he exclaimed, 'and I should be so grateful to anyone that I knew had shown kindness to him; and now I have been all over the town to get bread for my soldiers, and there is none to be had!' Mother Prioress' kind heart was touched, and telling the good man to keep his money, she gave him the loaves as well, with which he soon vanished out of the door, Edmund grumbling all the time because the nuns (and himself) had been deprived of their supper. Mother Prioress, laughing, told him the soldiers needed it more than we. She turned away, thinking over what she could possibly give the community for supper. She went— almost mechanically—to the bread-bin, where, lifting up the lid, she felt round in the dark. What was her delight to find two loaves which still remained, and which had to suffice for supper—as well as break-fast next morning.

We retired to rest, feeling we were, at any rate, well guarded; and the firm tread of the sentries, as they passed under our windows at regular intervals, inspired us with very different feelings from those we had experienced the week before, on hearing the heavy footsteps of the German watch.

The officials of the British Headquarters entered the town with the army, and for several weeks Ypres was their chief station, from which issued all the commands for the troops in the surrounding districts. We were not long, however, in knowing the consequences of such an honour. The next day, at about 10.30 a.m., the whirr of an aeroplane was heard. We were becoming accustomed to such novelties, and so did not pay too much attention, till, to our horror, we heard a volley of shots from the Grand' Place saluting the new-comer. We knew from this what nationality the visitor was. The firing continued for some time, and then ceased. What had happened? Our enclosure prevented us from following the exciting events of those troubled times, but friends usually kept us supplied with the most important news.

It was thus that, soon afterwards, we heard the fate of the air mon-ster which had tried to spy into what was happening within our walls. The first shots had been unsuccessful; but at last two struck the ma-chine, which began rapidly to descend. The inmates, unhurt, flew for their lives as soon as they touched ground; but, seizing the first motorcar to hand, the soldiers chased them, and at last took them prisoners. What was their horror to find in the aeroplane a plan of the town of Ypres, with places marked, on which to throw the three bombs, one of these places being the Grand' Place, then occupied by thousands of British soldiers.

Endless were the thanksgivings which mounted up to heaven for such a preservation, and prayers and supplications for Divine protection were redoubled. Since the beginning of the war, everyone, even the most indifferent, had turned to God, from Whom alone they felt that succour could come; and those who before never put their foot in church were now amongst the most fervent. Pilgrimages and processions were organised to turn aside the impending calamity; and, heedless of human respect, rich and poor, the fervent and the indifferent, raised their voices to the Mother of God, who has never yet been called upon in vain. Even the procession of Our Lady of Thuyn—so well known to all those who yearly flock to Ypres for the first Sunday in August—with its groups, its decorations, its music, had been turned into a penitential procession; and the 'Kermess' and other festivities, which took place during the following eight days, were prohibited. Needless to say, the monastery was not behindhand.

Every day the community assembled together at 1 o'clock for the recitation of the rosary, and, when possible, prayed aloud during the different employments of the day. Numberless were the aspirations to the Sacred Heart, Our Lady of Angels, Our Holy Father St. Benedict, each one's favourite patron, the Holy Angels, or the Souls in Purgatory. Each suggested what they thought the most likely to inspire devotion. Perhaps the best of all was that which Dame Josephine—*Requiescat in Pace*—announced to us one day at recreation. It ran as follows:

Dear St. Patrick, as you once chased the serpents and venomous reptiles out of Ireland, please now chase the Germans out of Belgium!

The Office of the Dead was not forgotten for those who had fallen on the battlefield, and we offered all our privations and sacrifices for the good success of the Allies, or the repose of the souls of the poor soldiers already killed. We also undertook to make badges of the Sacred Heart for the soldiers, though at the moment we saw no possible means of distributing them. At length, to our great joy, the arrival of the British troops, among whom were many Irish Catholics, opened an apostolate for us, which went on ever increasing. The idea had first

29

come to us when, weeks before, a number of Belgian soldiers were announced, of whom 250 were to have been quartered at the college. Reverend Mother Prioress had then suggested that we should make badges, so as at least to help in some little way, when everyone else seemed to be doing so much. We set to work with good will—some cutting the flannel—others embroidering—others writing—till at last we had finished. What was our disappointment to hear that not a single soldier had come to the college.

We then tried, in every way possible, to find a means of distributing our handiwork; but all in vain, till one day, a poor girl, called Hélène, who washed the steps and outer porch leading to the principal entrance of the convent, came to beg prayers for her brother who was at the front. Mother Prioress promised her we should all pray for her brother, at the same time giving her a badge of the Sacred Heart for him, together with a dozen others for anyone else she might know to be in the same position. Hélène soon returned for more, and the devotion spreading through the town, everyone came flocking to the parlour to get badges for a father, a brother, a cousin, a nephew at the front, many even also asking them for themselves, so that they might be preserved from all danger. Even the little children in the streets came, to ask for 'a little heart!' until the poor sister at the door was unable to get through her other work, owing to the constant ringing of the bell. In despair, she laid her complaints before her Superior, saying that a troop of children were there again, of whom one had come the first thing in the morning for a badge. On receiving it she had gone outside, where, changing hats with another child, she promptly returned, pretending to be someone else.

The sister, who had seen the whole performance through the *guichet*, had smiled at her innocent trick, and given her another. But now here she was again, this time with someone else's apron on, and bringing half a dozen other children with her. Mother Prioress then saw the little girl herself, who, nothing abashed, put out her hand saying, '*Des petits coeurs, s'il vous plaît, ma Soeur!*' This was too much for Mother Prioress' tender heart, and, instead of scolding, she told them there was nothing ready then; but for the future, if they came back on Mondays, they might have as many '*petits coeurs*' as they wished. The little troop marched quite contentedly out of the door, headed by the girl—who could not have been more than seven years old—and diminishing in size and age down to a little mite of two, who toddled out, hanging on to his brother's coat. The devout procession was brought up by a tiny black dog, which seemed highly delighted with the whole proceeding.

This little digression has brought us away from our subject, but was perhaps necessary to show how we were able to send badges to the soldiers, by means of this somewhat strange manner of apostolate; for a young girl, hearing of the devotion, brought them by dozens to St. Peter's parish (where an Irish regiment was stationed), impressing on each man, as she pinned the badge to his uniform, that it was made by 'the Irish Dames!'

CHAPTER 3

Incidents of the Struggle

Meanwhile, in the distance, we could hear the sound of cannon-ading, which told us of the approach of the enemy; and when we met at recreation, the one and only topic of conversation was the war. Each day brought its item of news—such or such a town had fallen, another was being bombarded, a village had been razed to the ground, another was burning, so many prisoners had been taken, such a number wounded, many alas! killed. As often as not, what we heard one day was contradicted the next, and what was confirmed in the morning as a fact, was flatly denied in the afternoon; so that one really did not know what to believe. We could at least believe our own ears, and those told us, by the ever-approaching sound of firing, that the danger was steadily increasing for the brave little town of Ypres. It was therefore decided that, in case of emergency, each nun should prepare a parcel of what was most necessary, lest the worst should come, and we should be obliged to fly.

Soon, crowds of refugees, from the towns and villages in the firing line, thronged the streets. The city was already crowded with soldiers. Where, then, could the refugees find lodging and nourishment? How were they to be assisted? All helped as far as they were able, and dinner and supper were daily distributed to some thirty or forty at the abbey doors. This meant an increase of work, which already weighed heavily enough on our reduced numbers; for we had, since September 8, lost four subjects—one choir dame and three lay-sisters—owing to the law then issued, commanding the expulsion of all Germans resident in Belgium. This had been the first shock. Nothing as yet foretold the future, nor gave us the least subject for serious alarm, when, on the afternoon of September 7, an official came to the parlour to acquaint us with the newly published law, and to say that our four German nuns would have to leave within thirty-six hours. We were literally stunned, Benedictines! Enclosed nuns! All over twenty-five years in the convent! What harm could they do? Surely no one could suspect them of being spies. Telegrams flew to Bruges, even to Antwerp, to obtain grace—all was useless, and at 3.30 p.m., September 8, we assisted at the first departure from the Abbey, which we innocently thought would be at the worst for about three weeks, little dreaming what we should still live to see.

These first poor victims were conducted by our chaplain to his lordship the Bishop of Bruges, who placed them in a convent just over the frontier in Holland, where we continued corresponding with them, until all communication was cut off by the arrival of the Germans, as has already been stated. In the result, we found our labours increased by the loss of our three lay-sisters; but we divided the work between us, and even rather enjoyed the novelty. Poor old Sister Magdalen (our oldest lay-sister), however, failed to see any joke in the business; and when she found herself once again cook, as she had been when she was young and active, her lamentations were unceasing. We tried to assist her, but she found us more in the way than anything else.

She discovered at last a consoler in the person of Edmund, who offered to peel apples, pears, and potatoes; and when the two could get together, Sister Magdalen poured forth the tale of her endless woes into Edmund's sympathetic ear, whilst he in return gave her the 'latest news'; and it was a curious spectacle to see the two together in the little court anxiously examining a passing aeroplane, to know of what nationality it was, though which of the pair was to decide the matter was rather questionable, Edmund being exceedingly short-sighted, and Sister Magdalen not too well versed in such learned matters.

To return to the refugees: Mother Prioress took some of us to help her in the children's refectory, and with her own hands prepared the food for them. For dinner they had a good soup, with plenty of boiled potatoes, bread, and beer: for supper, a plateful of porridge in which we mixed thin slices of apple, which made a delicious dish, and then potatoes in their jackets, bread, and beer. We had to work hard, for it was no small task to get such a meal ready for about forty starving persons. We left Sister Magdalen to grumble alone in the kitchen over the mysterious disappearance of her best pots and pans; especially one evening, when, forgetting to turn the appetising mixture which was preparing for supper, we not only spoilt the porridge, but burnt a hole in a beautiful copper saucepan.

The sound of hostilities came ever nearer and nearer. Dreadful rumours were current of an important battle about to be fought in the proximity of Ypres. What made things worse was the great number of spies that infested the neighbourhood. Daily they were arrested, but yet others managed to replace them. Four soldiers and one civilian kept a vigilant watch on the town, examining everyone who seemed the least suspicious, as much as the prisoners themselves.

Roulers, Warneton, Dixmude, and countless other towns and villages had succumbed; and at last, to our great grief, news reached us that the Germans were in Bruges, and had taken possession of the Episcopal palace—and our much-loved bishop, where was he? Alas! we were doomed not to hear, for all communication was cut off, and for the future we only knew what was happening in and around Ypres. And was it not enough? The windows already shook with the heavy firing. The roar of the guns in the distance scarcely stopped a moment. From the garret windows, we could already see the smoke of the battle on the horizon; and to think that, at every moment, hundreds of souls were appearing before the judgment-seat of God! Were they prepared? Terrifying problem!

As everywhere else, the German numbers far exceeded those of the Allies. It consequently came to pass that the latter were forced to retreat. It was thus that on Wednesday, October, 21, we received the alarming news that the town would probably be bombarded in the evening. We had already prepared our parcels in case we should be obliged to fly and now we were advised to live in our cellars, which were pronounced quite safe against any danger of shells or bombs. But our dear Lady Abbess, how should we get her down to the cellar, when it was only with great difficulty that she could move from one room to another? If we were suddenly forced to leave, what then would she do? We could only leave the matter in God's hands. We carried down a carpet, bed, armchair, and other things, to try to make matters as comfortable as possible for her—then our own bedding and provisions.

The precious treasures and antiquities had already been placed in security, and we now hastened to collect the remaining books and statues, which we hoped to save from the invaders. We had also been advised to pile up sand and earth against the cellar windows to deaden the force of the shells should they come in our direction. But if this were the case, they would first encounter the provision of *pétrole* in the garden—and then we should all be burnt alive. To prepare for this

34

alarming contingency, Dame Teresa and Dame Bernard, armed with spades, proceeded to the far end of the garden, where they dug an immense hole, at the same time carrying the earth to block the entrances to the different cellars. After a whole day's hard labour, they succeeded in finishing their excavation and in tilting the huge barrel, which they could neither roll nor drag—it being both too full and too heavy—to the place prepared. Their labour, however, proved all in vain; for Edmund, displeased at the barrel's disappearance, then highly amused at the brilliant enterprise, declared he could not draw the *pétrole* unless put back in its old position.

The reported fortunate arrival of a large number of Indian troops (they said 400,000, though 40,000 would be nearer the mark) had a reassuring effect: but we still remained in suspense, for if the Allies came by thousands, the Germans had a million men in the neighbourhood. The Allies and Germans also sustained frightful losses. The ambulance cars continually brought in the unfortunate victims from the battlefield, till at last the town was full to overflowing. One Sunday morning, a French officer and military doctor came to visit the convent to see if it would not be possible to place their wounded with us. We willingly offered our services, and Mother Prioress showing them the class-rooms, it was decided that the whole wing facing the ramparts, including the classrooms, children's dormitory and refectory, the library, noviceship and work-room, should be emptied and placed at their disposal. The great drawback was the lack of bedding; for already, before the arrival of the Germans in the town, we had given all we could possibly spare for the Belgian wounded, who had at that time been transported to Ypres.

The two gentlemen took their leave, very pleased with their visit, the officer—who seemed to all appearances a fervent Catholic—promising to send round word in the afternoon, when all should be decided. Despite the fact that it was Sunday, we listened (after having obtained permission) to the proverb, 'Many hands make light work,' and soon the rooms in question were emptied of all that would not serve for the soldiers, and were ready for their use. What was our disappointment, in the afternoon, to hear that the French officer, thanking us profusely for our offer, had found another place, which was more suitable, as being nearer the site of the engagement. We had always shown our goodwill, and were only too pleased to help in any little way the brave soldiers, who daily, nay hourly, watered with their blood Belgium's unfortunate soil.

This was not the last we heard of the officer; for we soon had a visit from a French deacon, who was serving as *infirmarian* at the ambulance, begging for bandages for the wounded soldiers. All our recreations and free moments were spent in 'rolling' bandages, for which were sacrificed sheets and veils, and in fact anything that could serve for the purpose—to all of which we of course added dozens of badges of the Sacred Heart. The deacon was overjoyed and returned several times 'to beg,' giving us news of the fighting. One day he brought a little souvenir, by way of thanks for our help. It consisted of a prayer-book found on a German wounded prisoner, who had died. The prayers were really beautiful, being taken mostly from passages of the Psalms, adapted for the time of war; while the soiled leaves showed that the book had been well read.

One afternoon, about this time, the sister who acted as *portress* announced the visit of an 'English Catholic priest,' serving as army chaplain. Mother Prioress went immediately round to the parlour to receive the reverend visitor, who stated that he had been charged by a well-known English lord, should he ever pass by Ypres, to come to our convent, to see the 'English flag' which one of his ancestors had sent to the abbey. Mother Prioress assured him that the only flag in the convent was the famous one captured by the Irish Brigade in the service of France at the Battle of Ramillies.[1] She added that she would be happy to give him a photograph of the flag. He said he would be enchanted, promising to call the next day to fetch it. Accordingly, the following day he returned, accompanied by two officers. Dame Josephine, together with Dame Teresa and Dame Patrick, were sent to entertain them.

On entering the parlour. Dame Josephine immediately knelt to receive the 'priest's' blessing, who looked rather put out at this un-wonted respect. After an interesting conversation on various topics, she asked how long he had been attached to the army. He said he had volunteered as chaplain, being in reality a monk, having also charge of a community of nuns. More and more interested at not only finding a 'priest' but a 'monk,' Dame Josephine expressed her admiration of the sacrifice he must have made in thus leaving his monastery, and asked to what Order he belonged. The reverend gentleman said that he was of the Order of St. John the Evangelist, and that he was indeed long-ing to be able to put on once more his holy habit.

---

1. See Note at end of chapter.

Then, making a sign to the officers, he abruptly finished the conversation, stating that he had an appointment, which he could by no means miss, and quickly vanished out of the parlour. Dame Teresa and Dame Patrick, who had hardly been able to keep in their laughter, now told Dame Josephine of her mistake; for they had truthfully divined that the supposed 'priest' was a Protestant clergyman. In fact he had stated on his introduction that he was 'a priest of the Church of England,' from which Dame Josephine had inferred that he was an 'English Catholic priest'; and so her special attention to him. Dame Teresa and Dame Patrick had rightly interpreted the visitor's description of himself as a Protestant clergyman, and enjoyed Dame Josephine's mistake.

Outside, the noise grew ever louder. The roar of the cannon, the rolling of the carriages, Paris omnibuses, provision and ambulance cars, the continual passage of cavalry and foot soldiers, and the motor-cars passing with lightning-like speed, made the quiet, sleepy little town of Ypres as animated as London's busiest streets. At night even the Allied regiments poured in, profiting by the obscurity to hide their movements from the Germans; while, contrasting with the darkness, the fire from the battlefield showed up clearly against the midnight sky. One evening, as we made our usual silent visit to the garrets before going to bed, a signal of alarm announced that something more than ordinary had occurred. In the distance thick clouds of smoke rose higher and higher, which, from time to time rolling back their dense masses, showed sheets of fire and flame. Were the Germans trying to set fire to the town? No one was near to enlighten us; so, anxious and uneasy, we retired to our cells, begging earnest help from Heaven. Since the first warning of bombardment one or other of us stopped up at night, being relieved after some hours, in case anything should happen while the community took their rest.

The most alarming news continued to pour in. The soldiers, by means of their telescopes, had descried two German aeroplanes throwing down *pétrole* to set the country and villages on fire. Were we to expect the same fate? Stories of German atrocities reached us from all quarters; but what moved us most was the account of the outrageous barbarities used upon women, even upon nuns.

We were far from an end of our troubles. Despite the danger and anxiety, we strove to keep up religious life, and the regular observances went on at the usual hours. Instead of distracting us, the roar of the battle only made us lift up our hearts with more fervour to God; and

it was with all the ardour of our souls that we repeated, at each succeeding hour of the Divine Office: '*Deus, in adjutorium meum intende!
Domine, ad adjuvandum me festina!*' The liturgy of Holy Mass, also—one
would have said it had been composed especially for the moment.

On Wednesday, October 28, between 1.30 and 2 p.m.—the hour
for our pious meditation—we were suddenly interrupted by a noise
to which we were not as yet accustomed. It seemed at first to be only
a cannon-ball, flying off on its deadly errand; but instead of growing
feebler, as the shell sped away towards the German ranks, the sound
and whirr of this new messenger of death grew ever louder and more
rapid, till it seemed, in its frightful rush, to be coming straight on our
doomed heads! Instinctively some flew to the little chapel of Our
Blessed Lady at one end of the garden; others remained still where
they were, not daring to move, till after a few seconds, which seemed
interminable, a deafening explosion told us that something dreadful
(alas! we knew not what) must have occurred.

We learned, afterwards, that it was the first of the bombs with
which the enemy, infuriated at the resistance of what they disdainfully
styled 'a handful of British soldiers,' determined to destroy the town
which they already feared they would never retake. The first bombs,
however, did no damage—the one which had so frightened us falling
into the moat which surrounds Ypres, behind the Church of St. James,
and two others just outside the town. At about 9.30 p.m., when we
were retiring to our cells after *matins*, another sound, far from musical, fell on our ears. As usual, some sped silently to the garrets, where,
though hearing strange noises, they could see nothing; so everyone
went to rest, concluding it was the sound of bombs again. In fact the
Germans were bombarding the town. We heard, the next day, that
several houses in the Rue Notre-Dame had been struck, and all the
windows in the street broken. The owners innocently sent for the
glazier to have the panes of glass repaired, little thinking that, in a few
weeks, scarce one window would remain in the whole of Ypres.

Not content with fighting on the ground, it seemed as though the
sky also would soon form a second battlefield. Aeroplanes passed at
regular hours from the town to the place of encounter, to bring back
news to the headquarters how the battle was waging. Besides this,
German Taubes made their appearance, waiting to seize their opportunity to renew, with more success than their first attempt, the disas-
trous ruin caused by the bombs. It was high time to think of our dear
Abbess' safety. It was therefore decided that she should take refuge at

Poperinghe, and Mother Prioress sent out for a carriage to convey her there; but in the general panic which reigned, every possible means of conveyance had been seized.

After several enquiries, a cab was at last secured, and soon drove up to the convent. Our dear Lady was so moved, when the news was broken to her, that four of us were obliged to carry her downstairs. After a little rest, we helped her to the carriage, which had driven round into the garden, to avoid the inconveniences which would necessarily have arisen had the departure taken place in the street. It proved almost impossible to get her into the carriage, owing to her inability to help herself. At length, thanks to the assistance of one of the Sisters of Providence, who had been more than devoted to her ever since her stroke, we succeeded; and accompanied by Dame Josephine, a Jubilarian, Dame Placid, and Sister Magdalen, our beloved abbess drove out of the enclosure,[2] the great door soon hiding her from our sight. Sad, troubled, and anxious, we turned back, wondering what would become of our dear absent ones. Would they arrive safely at their destination? Would they find kind faces and warm hearts to welcome them? Only the boom of the guns mockingly answered our silent enquiries.

NOTE:— THE 'FLAG' AT YPRES
By R. Barry O'Brien

There is a 'legend' of a 'blue flag' said to have been carried or captured by the Irish Brigade at the Battle of Ramillies, and which was subsequently deposited in the Irish convent at Ypres. This is a sceptical age. People do not believe unless they see; and I wished to submit this 'blue flag' to the test of ocular demonstration. Accordingly, in the autumn of 1907, I paid a visit to the old Flemish town, now so familiar to us all in its misfortunes. I was hospitably received by the kind and cheerful nuns who answered all my questions about the flag and the convent with alacrity. 'Can I see the flag?'—'Certainly.' And the 'flag' was sent for. It turned out not to be a blue flag at all. Blue was only part of a flag which, it would seem, had been originally blue, red, and yellow. An aged Irish nun described the flag as she had first seen it.

It was attached to a stick, and I remember reading on a slip of paper which was on the flag "*Remerciements* Refuged at Ypres, 170. . " The flag consisted of three parts—blue with a harp, red

2. By the Constitution of the Order, the enclosure may be broken in times of war, and in other cases provided for.

with three lions, and yellow. The red and yellow parts were accidentally destroyed, and all that remains is the blue, as you see it, with a harp; and we have also preserved one of the lions. The story that has come down to us is that it was left here after the battle of Ramillies I think, but whether it was the flag of the Irish Brigade, or an English flag captured by them at the battle, I do not know.

The flag, of course—blue with a harp, red with three lions, and yellow—suggests the royal standard of England, with a difference. At the time of the battle of Ramillies, the royal standard, or 'King's Colour,' consisted of four quarterings: the first and fourth quarters were subdivided, the three lions of England being in one half, the lion of Scotland in the other. The *fleurs-de-*lis were in the second quarter; the Irish harp was in the third.[3] But this (the Ypres) flag had, when the nun saw it, only three quarters—blue with harp, red with three lions, and yellow; the rest had then been apparently destroyed.

At the famous battle of 1706, the Irish Brigade was posted in the village of Ramillies. They fought with characteristic valour, giving way only when the French were beaten in another part of the field. The brigade was commanded by Lord Clare, who was mortally wounded in the fight. Charles Forman writes, in a letter published in 1735:—

At Ramillies we see Clare's regiment shining with trophies and covered with laurels even in the midst of a discomfited routed army. They had to do with a regiment which, I assure you, was neither Dutch nor German, and their courage precipitated them so far in pursuit of their enemy that they found themselves engaged at last in the throng of our army, where they braved their fate with incredible resolution. If you are desirous to know what regiment it was they engaged that day, the colours in the cloister of the Irish nuns at Ypres, which I thought had been taken by another Irish regiment, will satisfy your curiosity.[4]

Mr. Matthew O'Conor, in his *Military Memoirs of the Irish Nation*, says:—

Lord Clare ... cut his way through the enemy's battalions, bearing down their infantry with matchless intrepidity. In the heroic effort to save his corps he was mortally wounded, and many of

---

3. *Enc. Brit.* 11th ed.
4. *Courage of the Irish Nation.*

his best officers were killed. His Lieutenant, Colonel Murrough O'Brien, on this occasion evinced heroism worthy of the name of O'Brien. Assuming the command, and leading on his men with fixed bayonets, he bore down and broke through the enemy's ranks, took two pair of colours from the enemy, and joined the rear of the French retreat on the heights of St. Andre.'

Forman does not state to what regiment the colours belonged. O'Callaghan, in his *History of the Irish Brigade*, quotes him as saying:

I could be much more particular in relating this action, but some reasons oblige me, in prudence, to say no more of it.

O'Conor says that the colours belonged to a celebrated English regiment. O'Callaghan is more precise. He says:—

According to Captain Peter Drake, of Drakerath, County of Meath (who was at the battle with Villeroy's army, in De Couriere's regiment), Lord Clare engaged with a Scotch regiment in the Dutch service, between whom there was a great slaughter; that nobleman having lost 289 private sentinels, 22 commissioned officers, and 14 sergeants; yet they not only saved their colours, but gained a pair from the enemy. This Scotch regiment in the Dutch service was, by my French account, "almost entirely destroyed"; and, by the same account, Clare's engaged with equal honour the "English Regiment of Churchill," or that of the Duke of Marlborough's brother. Lieutenant-General Charles Churchill, and then commanded by its colonel's son, Lieutenant-Colonel Charles Churchill. This fine corps, at present the 3rd Regiment of Foot, or the Buffs, signalized itself very much in the action with another, or Lord Mordaunt's, "by driving three French regiments into a morass, where most of them were either destroyed or taken prisoners." But the "*Régiment Anglois de Churchill,*" according to the French narrative, fared very differently in encountering the Regiment of Clare, by which its colours were captured, as well as those of the "*Régiment Hollandois,*" or "Scotch regiment in the Dutch service."

The question may, or may not, be problematical, but it seems to me that what I saw in the convent at Ypres was a remnant of one of the flags captured, according to the authorities I have quoted, by the Irish Brigade at the Battle of Ramillies; and that flag was, apparently, the 'King's Colour' which reproduces the royal standard.

CHAPTER 4

In the Cellars

We were soon recalled from our reflections; for Mother Prioress, emerging from the parlour, announced to us that we were to have visitors that night. Two priests and five ladies had begged to be allowed to come to sleep in our cellars, as news had been brought that the Germans might penetrate into the town that very evening. One could not refuse at such a moment, though the idea was a novel one—enclosed nuns taking in strangers for the night. But in the face of such imminent peril, and in a case of life or death, there was no room for hesitation. So to work we set, preparing one cellar for the priests, and another for the ladies. In the midst of dragging down carpets, armchairs mattresses, the news soon spread that there was word from Poperinghe. We all crowded round Mother Prioress in the cellar, where, by the light of a little lamp, she endeavoured in vain to decipher a letter which Dame Placid had hurriedly scribbled in pencil, before the driver left to return to Ypres.

The picture was worth painting! Potatoes on one side, mattresses and bolsters on the other—a carpet half unrolled—each of us trying to peep over the other's shoulder, and to come as near as possible to catch every word. But alas! these latter were few in number and not reassuring. 'We can only get one room for Lady Abbess. . . . Everywhere full up. . . . We are standing shivering in the rain. . . . Please send ——' Then followed a list of things which were wanting. Poor Lady Abbess! Poor Dame Josephine! What was to be done? Mother Prioress consoled us by telling us she would send the carriage back the first thing next morning to see how everyone was, and to take all that was required. We then finished off our work as quickly as possible, and retired to our own cellar to say *compline* and *matins*; for it was already 10 o'clock. After this we lay down on our 'straw-sacks'—no one un-

D. Patrick.   D. Columban.   D. Bernard.   D. Teresa.   D. Walburge.

D. Placid.   Mother Prioress.   D. Aloysius.

THE IRISH DAMES OF YPRES

dressed. Even our 'refugees' had brought their packages with them, in case we should have to fly during the night. Contrary to all expectations, everything remained quiet—even the guns seemed to sleep. Was it a good or evil omen? Time would show.

At 5 o'clock next morning the alarm-clock aroused the community, instead of the well-known sound of the bell. There was no need, either, of the accustomed '*Domine, labia mea aperies*' at each cell door. At 5.30, we repaired to the choir as usual for meditation, and at 6 recited *lauds—prime* and *tierce*. At 7, the conventual Mass began; when, as though they had heard the long-silent bell, the guns growled out, like some caged lion, angry at being disturbed from its night's rest. The signal given, the battle waged fiercer than before, and the rattling windows, together with the noise resounding through the church and choir, told that the silence of the night had been the result of some tactics of the Germans, who had repulsed the Allies. Day of desolation, greater than we had before experienced! Not because the enemy was nearer, not because we were in more danger, but because, at the end of Holy Mass, we found ourselves deprived of what, up till then, had been our sole consolation in our anguish and woe. The sacred species had been consumed—the tabernacle was empty. The sanctuary lamp was extinguished. The fear of desecration had prompted this measure of prudence, and henceforth our daily Communion would be the only source of consolation, from which we should have to derive the courage and strength we so much needed.

The Germans nearer meant greater danger; so, with still more ardour, we set to work, especially as we were now still more reduced in numbers. The question suddenly arose, 'Who was to prepare the dinner?' Our cook, as has already been said, had been one of the three German sisters who had left us on September 8; subsequently, Sister Magdalen had replaced her, and she, too, now was gone. After mature deliberation. Dame Columban was named to fulfil that important function. But another puzzle presented itself—What were we to eat? For weeks, no one had seen an egg! Now, no milk could be got. Fish was out of the question—there was no one left to fish. To complete the misery, no bread arrived, for our baker had left the town. Nothing remained but to make some small loaves of meal, and whatever else we could manage—with potatoes, oatmeal, rice, and butter (of which the supply was still ample), adding apples and pears in abundance. Edmund was sent out to see if he could find anything in the town. He returned with four packets of Quaker oats, saying that that was all he could find, but that we could still have a hundred salted herrings if we wished to send for them.

We had just begun the cooking, when the tinkling of the little bell called everyone together, only to hear that a German Taube was sailing just over the abbey; so we were all ordered down to the cellars, but before we reached them there was *crack! crack! bang! bang!* and the rifle-shots flew up, from the street outside the convent, to salute the unwelcome visitor. But to no purpose, and soon the sinister whistling whirr of a descending projectile grated on our ears, while, with a loud crash, the bomb fell on some unfortunate building. We had at first been rather amused at this strange descent to our modern catacombs; but we soon changed our mirth to prayer, and aspiration followed aspiration, till the ceasing of the firing told us that the enemy was gone. We then emerged from the darkness, for we had hidden in the excavation under the steps leading up to the entrance of the monastery, as the surest place of refuge, there being no windows.

This was repeated five or six times a day; so we brought some work to the cellars to occupy us. The firing having begun next morning before breakfast was well finished, one sister arrived down with tea and bread and butter. Later on, while we were preparing some biscuits, the firing started again; so we brought down the mixing-bowl, ingredients and all. We continued our work and prayers and paid no more attention to the bombs or the rifle-shots.

Our dear Lady Abbess was not forgotten. The next day Mother Prioress sent for the carriage, while we all breathed a fervent 'Deo gratias' that our aged abbess was out of danger; for what would she have done in the midst of all the bombs? Owing to the panic, which was now at its height, all the inhabitants who were able were leaving the town, abandoning their houses, property—all, all—anxious only to save their lives. There was no means of finding a carriage.

Our life, by this time, had become still more like that of the Christians of the first era of the Church, our cellars taking the place of the catacombs, to which they bore some resemblance. We recited the Divine Office in the provision cellar under the kitchen, which we had first intended for Lady Abbess. A crucifix and statue of Our Lady replaced the altar. On the left were huge wooden cases filled with potatoes, and one small one of turnips—on the right, a cistern of water, with a big block for cutting meat (we had carefully hidden the hatchet, in case the Germans, seeing the two together, should be inspired to chop off our heads). Behind us, other cases were filled with

45

boxes and sundry things, whilst on top of them were the bread-bins. We were, however, too much taken up with the danger we were in to be distracted by our surroundings. We realised then, to the full, the weakness of man's feeble efforts, and how true it is that God alone is able to protect those who put their trust in Him.

The cellar adjoining, leading up to the kitchen, was designed for the refectory. In it were the butter-tubs, the big meat-safe, the now empty jars for the milk. A long narrow table was placed down the centre, with our serviettes, knives, spoons, and forks; while everyone tried to take as little space as possible, so as to leave room for her neighbour. The procession to dinner and supper was rather longer than usual, leading from the ante-choir through the kitchen, scullery, down the cellar stairs, and it was no light work carrying down all the 'portions,' continually running up and down the steps, with the evident danger of arriving at the bottom quicker than one wanted to, sending plates and dishes in advance.

Time was passing away, we now had to strip the altar—to put away the throne and tabernacle. Someone suggested placing the tabernacle in the ground, using a very large iron boiler to keep out the damp, and thus prevent it from being spoilt. This plan, however, did not succeed, as will be seen. Dame Teresa and Dame Bernard flew off to enlarge the pit they had already begun, watching all the time for any Taube which might by chance drop a bomb on their heads, and, indeed, more than once, they were obliged to take refuge in the abbey. Strange to say, these things took place on Sunday, the Feast of All Saints. It was rather hard work for a holiday of obligation, but we obtained the necessary authorisation. Towards evening the hole was finished and the boiler placed in readiness. But how lift the throne, which took four men to carry as far as the inner sacristy?

First we thought of getting some workmen, but were any still in the town? No, we must do it ourselves. So, climbing up, we gradually managed to slip the throne off the tabernacle, having taken out the altar-stone. We then got down; and whether the angels, spreading their wings underneath, took part of the weight away or not, we carried it quite easily to the choir, where, resting it on the floor, we enveloped the whole in a blanket which we covered again with a sheet. The tabernacle was next taken in the same manner, and, reciting the '*Adoremus*,' '*Laudate*,' '*Adoro Te*,' we passed with our precious load through the cloisters into the garden. It was a lovely moonlight night, and our little procession, winding its way through the garden paths, reminded us of the Levites carrying away the tabernacle, when attacked by the Philistines. We soon came to the place, where the two 'Royal Engineers'—for so they had styled themselves (Dame Teresa and Dame Bernard)—were putting all their strength into breaking an iron bar in two, a task which they were forced to abandon.

We reverently placed our burden on the edge of the cauldron, but found it was too small. Almost pleased at the failure, we once more shouldered the tabernacle, raising our eyes instinctively to the dark blue sky, where the pale autumn moon shone so brightly, and the cry of '*Pulchra ut luna*' escaped from our lips, as our hearts invoked the aid of Her, who was truly the tabernacle of the Most High. As we gazed upwards, where the first bright stars glittered among the small fleecy clouds, wondering at the contrast of the quiet beauty of the heavens and the bloodshed and carnage on earth, a strange cloud, unlike its smaller brethren, passed slowly on. It attracted our attention.

In all probability it was formed by some German shell which had burst in the air and produced the vapour and smoke which, as we looked, passed gradually away. We then re-formed our procession and deposited the tabernacle in the chapter-house for the night. Needless to say, it takes less time to relate all this than it did to do it, and numberless were the cuts, blows, scrapes, and scratches, which we received during those hours of true 'hard labour'; but we were in time of war, and war meant suffering, so we paid no attention to our bruises.

Our fruitless enquiries for a means to get news of Lady Abbess were at last crowned with success. Hélène, the poor girl of whom mention has been already made, and who now received food and help from the monastery, came, on Sunday afternoon, to say that two of her brothers had offered to walk to Poperinghe next day, and would take whatever we wished to send. After *matins*, Mother Prioress made up two big parcels, putting in all that she could possibly think of which might give pleasure to the absent ones. The next day was spent in expectation of the news we should hear when the young men returned.

Breakfast was not yet finished, when the *portress* came in with a tale of woe. One of our workmen was in the parlour, begging for help. During the night a bomb had been thrown on the house next to his; and he was so terrified that, not daring to remain in his own house any more, he had come with his wife and four little children to ask a lodging in our cellars. For a moment Reverend Mother hesitated; but her kind heart was too moved to refuse, and so the whole family went down into the cellar underneath the classroom, which was separated from the rest, and there remained as happy as could be. We were soon to feel the truth of the saying of the gospel, '*What you give to the least of My little ones, you give it unto Me.*'

In the afternoon, we heard that the cab-driver, who had been to the convent on Friday, had spread the news that he had been ordered to Poperinghe the next day, to bring back the Lady Abbess and nuns. What had happened? Could they not remain in their lodgings? Did they think that the bombardment had stopped—just when it was raging more fiercely than ever—when, every day, we thought we should be obliged to flee ourselves? They must be stopped—but how? Hélène, who was again sent for, came announcing her two brothers' return. Mother Prioress asked if it would be too much for them to go back to Poperinghe to stop Lady Abbess from returning. They, however, declared they would never undertake it again, the danger being too great, and it being impossible to advance among the soldiers. Mother Prioress then determined to go herself, asking Hélène if she would be afraid to go with her to show the way. Hélène bravely replied that she was not afraid and would willingly accompany Mother Prioress.

As usual, Mother Prioress would allow none of us to endanger our lives. She would go herself—and on foot, as the price demanded for the only carriage available was no less than 40 francs. In vain we begged her to let one of us go. It was to no purpose; and on Tuesday morning she started off, accompanied by Hélène, leaving the community in a state of anxiety impossible to describe. 'Would she be able to walk so far?' we asked ourselves. 'What if a bomb or shell were to burst on the road?' 'Would she not probably miss Lady Abbess' carriage?' We were now truly orphans, deprived both of our abbess and our prioress, and not knowing what might happen to either of them. After an earnest '*Sub tuum*' and '*Angeli, Archangeli*,' we went about our different tasks; for we had promised Reverend Mother to be doubly fervent in her absence. At 11 o'clock we said the office and afterwards sat down to dinner, for which no one felt the least inclined. The latter was not yet finished, when there was a ring at the doorbell, and in a few moments our prioress stood before us. We could hardly believe our eyes. She then related her adventures which, for more accuracy, I give from her own notes:—

When I heard the door shutting behind me, and the key turning in the lock, in spite of all my efforts, the tears came to my eyes. I was then really out of the enclosure—back again in the world— after twenty-seven years spent in peaceful solitude. The very sight of the steps brought back the memory of the day when I mounted them to enter the monastery. I hesitated . . . There was still only the door between us, but no! my duty lay before me. I must prevent Lady Abbess returning; so, taking courage, I started off with Hélène, who was trying all she could to console me. I followed her blindly. As we advanced, the traffic increased more and more. Motorcars, cavalry, foot-soldiers, cyclists, passed in rapid succession.

On the pavement, crowds of fugitives blocked the passage. Old and young, rich and poor, alike were flying, taking only a few small packets with them—their only possessions. Mothers, distracted with grief, led their little ones by the hand, while the children chattered away, little knowing the misery which perhaps awaited them. And the soldiers! they never ceased. The Allies, in their different uniforms, passed and repassed in one continued stream, while the motor-cars and bicycles deftly wended their way between soldiers and civilians. I was stupefied, and thought at every moment we should be run over; but my companion, amused at my astonishment, assured me there was nothing to fear. We had called on the *burgomaster* for our passports; but he was absent, and we had been obliged to go to the town hall.

After that, I called on *M. le Principal du College Episcopal*, our chaplain, to state that it was impossible to obtain a carriage (as I had arranged with him that morning), owing to our poverty, and that I should therefore be obliged to go on foot. He approved of our undertaking, and even advised me to take the whole community straight away to Poperinghe. I told him I must first prevent Lady Abbess from coming back; but that, once at Poperinghe, I intended certainly to look out for a convent which would receive us all. The British ambulance was established in the college, and it seemed really like barracks.

Once in the street again, I heard, *click! clack!!* the British soldiers were shooting at a German Taube passing over the town. We hastened on. Many houses were already empty—nearly all the shops were closed. Here and there a heap of ruins showed where a shell had made its way, while out of the broken windows, the curtains blowing in the wind showed the remains of what had once been sumptuous apartments. We soon left the station behind us, and continued on the main road, with here and there a few houses which seemed more safe by being out of the town; yet some of them had also been struck. The regiments filled the road more numerously than ever, while the unfortunate fugitives, with a look of terror on their pale faces, fled from the doomed city.

Some, who had left days before, were venturing back again in the hope of finding their homes still untouched. We continued our way, stopped now and then by some unfortunate creature, asking where we were going, and relating in return his story of woe. Suddenly I heard myself called by name. "Dame Maura! Yes, it is really she!" and, at the same moment, Marie Tack (an old pupil) flew into my arms.

Her brother, who accompanied her, now came forward, and took great interest in everything concerning the convent. "Well!" he said, "we are benefactors of the Carmelites at Poperinghe—my brother even gave them their house. Say that it is I who have sent you, and you will surely be well received." I thanked him for his kindness and we parted, they returning to Ypres, where they had not dared to sleep. In my heart I sent a grateful aspiration towards the Divine Providence of God, which thus gave me this little ray of hope. Meanwhile, the parcels we were carrying began to weigh more and more heavily on us. We helped each other as best we could, as I saw that poor Hélène was almost out of breath, having taken the heaviest for herself.

The roads also were very bad, and we could hardly advance owing to the mud. At length, after walking two hours, we saw the steeple of Vlamertinghe in the distance. It was time, for I felt I could not go farther. I remembered that Louise Veys (another old pupil) lived at Vlamertinghe, though I had forgotten the address. I asked several people in the streets if they could direct me, but I received always the same answer: "I am sorry not to be able to oblige you, Sister. I am a stranger, I come from Ypres— from Roulers—from Zonnebeke."

At last, I ventured to ring at the door of one of the houses. It happened to be the very one I was looking for. Louise, who was at the ambulance, came running to meet me, with Mariette and Germaine Tyberghein, and Marie-Paule Vander Meersch. The latter told me that the church of their village, Langemarck, was burnt, and she feared that their house, which was close by, would have met with the same fate. At this moment, her sister Claire, who had remained with the wounded soldiers, came running in, crying out: "Lady Abbess is here, and Dame Josephine."

"Where?" I exclaimed. Instead of answering, she took me by the hand, and we both ran out to where a cab was standing. I flew to the door, and was soon in Lady Abbess' arms. I could hardly restrain my tears. How was it then that the carriage on its way from Poperinghe to Ypres had stopped just in front of the Veys' house, when neither the driver nor anyone else knew to whom it belonged, or still less that I was there? Once again Divine Providence had come to our help, otherwise we should have missed each other. The cabman, who had innocently been the means of our happy meeting, by stopping to get refreshments, now appeared. I explained that it was an act of the greatest imprudence to conduct Lady Abbess to Ypres; but he would listen to nothing—meaning to go. He declared the danger was far greater at Poperinghe, and then drove away with Mother Abbess to Ypres, leaving me in consternation.

Mariette and Germaine Tyberghein offered me their carriage, to return to Ypres. It was soon ready, and we started back once more. Halfway to Ypres, we saw the other cab again stationary, and a British officer talking to the nuns through the window. We called out to our coachman to stop, knocking at the window with might and main. All was useless. The noise of the innumerable horses, provision and ammunition carts, passing, deafened him, and he continued peacefully, quite unaware that anything had happened. When we arrived at Ypres, the Germans were shelling it in real earnest. I wished to go back again, to stop Lady Abbess at any price, but was not allowed. They said no one would be permitted to come into the town, and that the other cab would probably have been sent back.'

This day was not to pass without another surprise; for what was our astonishment, at about eight o'clock, to see Dame Placid once more in our midst! The officer whom Mother Prioress had seen talking through the carriage-window, had said that on no account could Lady Abbess think of going on to Ypres, which was actually being bombarded. The cab had thereupon gone back to Poperinghe; but Dame Placid had alighted, and come to Ypres on foot. We crowded round her to get news of all that had happened during the last four days, which seemed like four weeks. After we had related all that had passed in the monastery since her departure. Dame Placid told us in return what she had gone through. On the Friday afternoon, when our poor refugees had driven to Poperinghe, they went straight to the Benedictine Convent, making sure they would be received without any difficulty. But alas! the monastery was full of soldiers, and no less than fifty other fugitives were waiting at the door. From there, they drove to the Soeurs Polains where, also, every corner was taken up— then they went on to a private house, but always with the same result, until at last some one directed them to La Sainte Union, where they found a lodging. It had been pouring rain the whole time, and they were all cramped and cold. Poor Lady Abbess missed so much the little comforts she had had at the abbey, and finally resolved to return to Ypres, with the result we know.

What could we now do to help her? It was decided that Sister Romana should go back with Dame Placid to see if she could not be of use. The two fugitives left at about 4 o'clock, pushing before them a kind of bath-chair filled with packets and parcels for Lady Abbess and the old nuns. A rather strange equipment, which was doomed never to reach its destination. Having, with the greatest difficulty—owing to the condition of the roads—arrived at Vlamertinghe, they were stopped by several regiments passing. They waited, waited, waited, till at last an officer, seeing their distress, gave a signal, and the soldiers halted to allow them to cross. Despairing of ever reaching Poperinghe with their load, they called at the house where Mother Prioress had been received that morning, and begged to leave the little carriage and its contents there. They then walked on more easily, and were able to get to Lady Abbess before nightfall.

CHAPTER 5

The Bombardment

To return to the abbey. Everything had become suddenly animated there; for, at the departure of Dame Placid and Sister Romana, Reverend Mother Prioress had declared that we should all follow, taking advantage of the occasion, as there was a cessation of hostilities for the moment. In vain some of us begged to be allowed to remain behind; but we had all to make our last preparations and go. When, however, the packages turned up, each bigger than the other, we looked at one another in dismay. How should we ever drag such a load with us? Dame Columban and Dame Bernard offered to try to find a workman to help us, and their offer was finally accepted. What happened they record.

Mother Prioress gave us her blessing, and let us out of the enclosure door. Oh dear! What a sensation! Happy prisoners for so many years, we now found ourselves in the streets. With a shudder, we started on our errand. We had not gone a hundred paces, when, *whizz . . . bang!* a shell passed over our heads; a moment after, *whizz . . . bang*, another—then another—and another. Halfway down the street, a British officer on horseback cried out to us: "*Mes Soeurs . . . . a la maison.*" Where were we to go? We knew no one. We looked round to find a place of refuge; and, seeing a man standing on his doorstep, timidly asked if we might take shelter there. He willingly agreed, seeming only too delighted to bid us welcome. As soon as the officer had vanished, we asked our kind host if he could tell us where the workman (Chinchemaillie) we were seeking lived, and on being directed to his abode, we left the house.

Once more in the street, we hurried on. While crossing the

Grand' Place, a perfect hail of shells and shrapnel came down on all sides. Explosion followed explosion. The soldiers and civilians crouched down by the side of the houses whenever a shell burst; but we, ignorant of the great risk we were running, walked bravely on. At length we concluded we must have taken a wrong turning; so, meeting a pale-faced gentleman, we asked him if he would be so kind as to put us on the right road again. He was hurrying along, burdened with parcels of all sizes, and carrying a jug of milk. When we spoke to him, he seemed almost dazed. "Yes, Sisters," he answered ". . . certainly . . . but . . . . . . the Germans have just shelled my house . . . I am running to save my life." We understood then why he looked so disturbed; offering our deepest sympathy, we begged him not to trouble. Recovering himself, he assured us that he was going our way, and would willingly accompany us. We took some of his parcels from him, and went along.

At a turning in the street we parted, having received further directions from him and thanked him for his kindness. Another man, having overheard our conversation, came forward, and offered to conduct us to the house in question. We went on, passing several buildings which had been much injured, and finally, the bombardment raging all the time, arrived at our destination, only to hear that the workman had left the town in the morning, and had not been able to re-enter it. The people of the house showed us the greatest kindness, especially on hearing who we were, and insisted on our spending the night in their cellar, saying it was far too dangerous to go out again.

We thanked them for their offer, but of course set off again for the monastery. Just as we arrived at the Grand' Place, Hélène, who had already rendered such valuable services to the community came running towards us. She was breathless and almost crying, having been searching for us everywhere; we had been out so long, and the bombardment had been so continuous, that the nuns thought we must have been killed. We soon got safely home, where we found everyone in a dreadful state of anxiety.

On hearing the continual explosions, Mother Prioress and the community had knelt down by the enclosure door, to pray for the safe return of Dame Columban and Dame Bernard. As they delayed so long. Reverend Mother sent Edmund to ask Hélène to look for them. Having done so, Edmund returned and did his best to persuade the nuns that there was no need to leave the abbey. 'You have your cellars to shelter you, why do you want to go? What will become of me, when you are gone? If a bomb falls on the convent, well, it will be the will of God. Why not die here as well as anywhere else?' We shall see later, that when the shell really did fall on the abbey, the good man was anything but resigned to die. As he perceived that he gained nothing by his eloquence, he went out into the street, and soon returned with a soldier, to see if the newcomer might not be more successful. The soldier was at first rather bewildered at his new surroundings, being an English Protestant, but was soon set at ease on finding that we talked English.

At this moment the two wanderers came back, and set everyone's heart at ease. Of course there was no longer a question of our leaving that night, especially as the soldier assured us that there was no danger that the Germans would get into Ypres, adding that our cellars would be proof against all their bombs. Edmund, by this time, was triumphant, and pulling out his cigar-case, offered it to the 'Tommy,' who insisted on his accepting a cigarette in return. Edmund then began to relate the story of his woes. 'What should I have to eat, if they were to go?' he exclaimed. 'Imagine, the other day the sister brought me my dinner. What did I see? I could hardly believe my eyes! A piece of beef-steak. I sat down in high glee; for I do not remember when I had had a piece before. What was my disappointment to find what I had taken to be a beef-steak was nothing else than a piece of fried brown bread. I could have thrown it in the fire.' The soldier then took his leave, though not before Mother Prioress had given him a badge of the Sacred Heart, which he promised to wear always as a souvenir of his visit to our abbey. We took care, also, to give him as many apples and pears as he could put into his pockets.

The number of people seeking shelter for the night in the convent increased constantly. Already, some thirty persons had come; some bringing their own mattresses, the others depending on our charity. We gave all that we had. In the end, no fewer than fifty-seven persons came for a night's lodging. Numberless poor came also during the day for food, for they could not find anything to eat in the town; bakers, butchers, grocers—all had fled to save their lives. We were in the greatest necessity ourselves, but still gave to all who asked. We experienced the truth of our Lord's words, '*Give, and you shall receive,*' when, a few days later, we were in the streets—without a house, without food, without money. It was then, indeed, that we received a hundredfold the charity we showed towards those who applied to us in their distress.

On the Wednesday morning, Our Lord gave us a little surprise. Our chaplain had been obliged to leave Ypres the evening before, to place the nuns who lived in his college in safety. But the Divine Master watched over us, and instead of the one Mass which we had lost. He sent us two French military priests to offer up the Holy Sacrifice for us. Reverend Mother presented her excuses for the poor breakfast they received—for we had nothing to give them but the bread which we had made ourselves out of meal, and some pears—asking their opinion of the situation. They strongly advised us to leave while there was yet time and enquired where we thought of going. Mother Prioress told them that the Lady Abbess of Oulton Abbey in England had offered, from the very outset of the war, to take the whole community, but the great question was how to get so far.

They said that we ought to apply to the British Command for help, expressing the opinion that the English ambulance, established at the college of which our chaplain was the President, would surely come to our assistance. They then left, saying how delightful it had been to have found such a peaceful spot in which to say Mass, after the noise and horrors to which they had been so long accustomed. The day passed slowly. The Germans were gaining ground. The noise of the Allied guns was now deafening. We were obliged to leave all the windows ajar, to prevent the glass being broken by the shocks, which made the house tremble from the garrets to the cellar. Monoplanes and biplanes, friendly and hostile, passed continually overhead—the former chasing the latter, which were dropping bombs without end on the town. At last, two friendly aeroplanes undertook to mount guard, and remained continually hovering round and round; but even then, the Taubes came; and the fighting went on in the air, as well as on all sides of us. The risks of remaining were certainly great; and yet—why leave our Abbey, when it was still untouched? We were sure of a warm welcome at Oulton; but how could the whole community get there, and, above all, our beloved Lady Abbess?

On the other hand, how were we to live in Ypres? Not only were we in danger of being killed at any moment, but there was no longer any means of getting food. For several days Edmund had, with the greatest difficulty, procured two pints of skimmed milk; but even this would soon cease. Again, there was certainly no more prospect of receiving any money in Belgium, where the banks had all been robbed. We had paid our debts prior to the commencement of hostilities; and so had very little money left. In the afternoon, Mother Prioress determined to go out and seek for information at the British Headquarters; for everyone seemed to have deserted the stricken town. She took Dame Columban and Dame Patrick with her. They went first to the college. At the end of the Rue St. Jacques, a French soldier gave a military salute and advanced towards them. It was one of the priests who had said Mass for the community in the morning. He accompanied the three nuns as far as the college, but told them that the ambulance had left during the night, which was a very bad sign; for when the wounded were removed, it showed that there was great danger. He also promised to attend the next morning at 5 o'clock to say Mass.

It was notified that the headquarters were to be found a mile and a half out of Ypres. The *burgomaster* had also left the town. Going to the houses of several influential people—M. and Mme. le Sénateur Fracy de Venbeck and Mme. Van den Berghe and others—friends of the monastery, Mother Prioress and her companions found them all locked up, and the inhabitants gone. One big shop was burning, and the French soldiers were trying to put the fire out. A baker's establishment had a large hole in the roof. It was pouring rain, and the nuns had no umbrella; so they turned their steps homewards. But their mission was not to prove useless; for Divine Providence had arranged that they were to help one of His poor creatures.

Having arrived at the Grand' Place, they were stopped by an English officer, who pointed to a cart, driven by a soldier, which was following them. In it was an old woman lying, apparently helpless. He explained to them that, passing by a deserted village, which had been destroyed by the Germans, he had found her lying in a ditch. He had lifted her into the cart and taken her along with him, and he now asked if the nuns could not direct him to some hospital or institute where she would be taken care of. They went with him as far as the hospice, where the officials declared they had more work than they could possibly attend to; still, as Mother Prioress begged so hard, they took her in.

The poor old woman was over ninety. How many are there who, like her, find themselves turned out of the little home, which had perhaps cost them their whole life's savings. Why should the poor, the aged, the infirm, the innocent, suffer to satisfy the ambition of the unjust? Truly, '*My ways are not your ways, saith the Lord.*' In eternity, lost in the blissful contemplation of God's infinite perfections, we shall understand the wisdom of those things which now surpass our poor intelligence.

On Thursday morning, we arose at 4.30 from what might truly be styled *'our humble couch,'* to be ready for the promised Mass at 5 o'clock. During the night, we had harboured the Sisters of Providence, who were leaving next day. Having waited half an hour, and no priest coming, we recited *lauds*, *prime*, and *tierce*. We again waited in all patience, but no one appeared. We could not miss Holy Mass and Communion—it was the only source of consolation left to us; besides, we never knew if, perhaps, we should live to see the following day. The regiment to which the priests belonged had probably been ordered off during the night—hence the reason of their non-arrival. At 7.30 Mother Prioress assembled us all at the enclosure door, and, leaving Edmund in charge of the convent, we put down our veils, and two by two, started for the Carmelite Convent, situated a little way down the street.

There we learned that the nuns had left the day before. We were determined not to miss Mass at any cost, so continued as far as the Church of St. James, where we arrived in the middle of one Mass, after which we received Holy Communion, and then had the happiness of assisting at another Mass—celebrated also by a French chaplain, though not one of those who had been at the abbey the day before. On our way home, we were met by a priest of the parish, who had served Mass for a long time in our chapel, when he was a young boy, and, returning to Ypres years after, had always remained attached to the community. He was touched to see us thus obliged to break our beloved enclosure, and spoke words of courage and consolation to us.

The day passed in great anxiety, relieved by one little incident, which, in spite of all our perils and troubles, afforded us amusement. Dame Columban, busy cooking in the kitchen, found no dishes coming from the scullery, where Sister Winefride now presided at the washing up. She looked in, asking when the things would be clean, and found the Sister, bending over a tub of boiling water, looking very tired and hot, and received an answer, that all would soon be finished. Some time passed, but no dishes came. Being at a loss to know the cause of the delay, she went once more to the scullery to enquire, and found things in exactly the same state as before. On asking what was wrong, Sister Winefride exclaimed, in a piteous tone of voice: 'Do you *really* think we are going this morning?'

'Of course not! who said so?'

'I don't know, but I thought perhaps we might; so, in order not to have too much to carry, I have put on two habits, two scapulars, two petticoats, and I *do* feel so hot! If I may just go to our cell and change, I think I'll get on better!' Having, as may easily be imagined, obtained the permission, she soon came joyfully back to her work.

We no longer believed the assurance the British soldiers gave us, that we were quite safe, and we now set to work to lighten our packages as much as possible, only taking what was strictly necessary; it being even decided that we should only take one breviary each, and leave the other three behind. There still remained a good deal to carry; for we were to take some provisions, not knowing if we should find refuge at Poperinghe, or if we should have to go straight to England. It was absolutely necessary to find some means of carrying our packages, were it but a wheelbarrow. Mother Prioress now found a reward for her charity, for the poor workman, whom she had so kindly received with his family in the cellar, hearing of our distress, found a handcart, and, what was more, promised to push it for us.

The next day, Friday, we went out again to Holy Mass in St. James's, having had very few people in the cellar, for all those who could possibly leave the town had already done so. When we returned. Mother Prioress announced her decision to go to the headquarters, and set off immediately, accompanied by Dame Patrick, without even taking her breakfast. The rest of the community went about their different occupations, until she should return. Nine o'clock struck, half-past nine, ten, half-past ten, still no Mother Prioress! To say we were anxious but feebly expresses our state of mind. The shells and bombs were flying in all directions; and the explosions—joined to the firing of the guns—resembled some huge machinery with its never-ceasing *boom* and *crash*. We prepared the dinner, which consisted of salt herrings and fried potatoes; but there was no account of the Mother Prioress as yet.

Each ring at the door made us crowd round in joyful expectation, but each time a disconsolate 'No' was all the answer we received from the *portress*. We recited *Sext* and *None*, but no Mother Prioress as yet! We consulted together as to what should be done. Some thought Reverend Mother must have been kept—others that she had perhaps found a motorcar, and had seized the opportunity to go to Poperinghe to see Lady Abbess. The dinner was spoiling on the fire, yet no one cared to sit down to eat. The bell rang, but we scarcely had the heart to answer it—-, we had been disappointed so often. We felt sure we should only hear another 'No.' Suddenly a joyous ringing of the little hand-bell, which had served alike to announce the Divine Office, and to warn us of German Taubes passing overhead, brought everyone to their feet, and we soon crowded round our dear prioress to beg her blessing, asking all together for an explanation of her long absence. For greater surety we shall cite her own notes:—

The headquarters had left the town, we had therefore a long way to go. In town, there was ever the same movement of troops, but the aspect seemed still more mournful. The shells had begun their work of destruction on the Grand' Place. A corner of the Halles had been struck. A house had received a bomb on the roof, which, penetrating the building, carried away half of the front, making its way through ceilings and floors, throwing the furniture to right and left, carrying chairs down into the very cellar. The people standing around were looking on aghast. We passed on, but soon a poor woman stopped us: "And you Sisters, from where do you come?"—"We are the Irish Dames of St. James's Street." "Oh yes! I know the convent well. Are you also leaving?"—"I am afraid we shall be obliged to do so!"—and we continued our walk. We had already turned off into another street, when we heard hurried steps behind us, and some one crying out: "Sisters, Sisters! *Zusters, Zusters!*"

It was the good woman again, with her kind face, her big handkerchief round her head, and her blue Flemish apron. "*Zuster!* Don't leave the town, come home with me, we are poor, but still you can have my house and all I have."—"Good woman," I said, taking her two hands, "thank you a thousand times, do not be anxious for us. Our Lord will take care of us." I could have kissed the dear creature then and there. We could not stop. Soon a crowd blocked our passage. "A shell struck here last night" they explained to us—it was the *Cercle Catholique*—"and penetrated into the cellar where a poor man had taken refuge with his three children, thinking he would be more protected here than in his own home, and there is his house (just two buildings farther on) untouched. The man has his hand off, two children are killed, and the third, a girl, is dying!"

By this time we had made our way through the crowd. The fugitives were continually passing, leaving homes and all behind. At length we arrived at the residence of the staff officers.

We explained our case to one of them, who received us very courteously, and who told us the best thing to do would be to address ourselves to General Sir Douglas Haig. An orderly informed him that Sir Douglas had left for Brielen. The officer advised us to go there. It was already 8.30, and we had still a good hour's walk before us. The road resembled that to Poperinghe. One must have seen the continual passage of troops, motorcars, horses, fugitives, in the narrow lanes, the roads inches thick with mud, to have a true idea of it.

Here and there a house struck by a shell, or bespattered with mud almost to the roof, gave an indescribable air of sadness to the surroundings; while a bouquet of flowers, or an odd *bibelot* discarded in a shop-window, remained as a last souvenir of the joys and prosperity of our brave little Belgium. Brielen now came in sight. We stopped before the Calvary, erected at the entrance to the cemetery, and then paid a visit to the church. On coming out, we met the *curé* of the village, who interested himself in our trials and sorrows.

We then asked the way to the headquarters, where we found it was impossible to see Sir Douglas. His *aide-de-camp* gave us some rather vague information, but kindly offered to get us seats in a motorcar that was leaving for Poperinghe. It did not start, however, till midday, and even then I could not go without telling the community at Ypres. We set out on our way back to Ypres. Just outside the village a poor woman, all in tears, stopped us, showing us a big cavity which a shell had just made in the ground by her farm. "I should have been killed," she exclaimed, "except for the brave English soldiers, who, seeing the shell coming in my direction, had just the time to take me up and push me into the farm, but my cow is gone! Our little farm was all our fortune!" and she wiped away the tears with a corner of her apron.

Poor dear! How many are there still more unfortunate than she! As we approached the town, the whistling shriek of the shells became more distinct; the Germans were bombarding Ypres as hard as they could. We found ourselves almost alone in the streets. Here and there a few soldiers remained in the doorways of the houses. A shell flew straight over us! What a protection of Divine Providence! A few steps off a building was struck, and we just escaped getting a shower of bricks and glass on top of us. "Come to the other side!" Dame Patrick called out. We crossed over, murmuring aspirations all the time.

A little farther on another shell burst, and the house we had just passed fell a heap of shapeless ruins. We hastened our steps to get out of the street, which seemed to be the chief point of attack. We then breathed more freely, till—arrived at the Grand' Place—we were welcomed by a regular shower of shells which flew in all directions. Happily we had almost reached our destination, though, had it not been for Dame Patrick, I should never have known my way, but should probably have passed by the monastery. At the door we met two brave Britishers whom I told to come into the parlour, where they would be more out of danger. They did not feel afraid, and said they were sent to search for some bread; for they could not get any in the town. I gave them some of the provisions which we were to take with us, with a little pot of butter, and—what I knew they liked so much—as many pears as they could carry. They were delighted, and so were we. We then talked of the war, and the old story came back again, the hope so cherished by all, and yet also not realised: "Oh! it will soon be over. We'll be home for Christmas!"

Our poor dinner was now served, the last we were to take in the dear old home. The reading was made aloud as usual. The subject was 'Holy Poverty'—truly appropriate for the times and surroundings. The last words which the reader pronounced before the signal was given, were: '*The Lord has given, the Lord has taken away! May His Holy Name be blessed!*' Had we prepared the reading beforehand, it could not have been better chosen. Our dear Lord had truly given us our abbey, and had made it withstand the course of years, with all the changes of government, wars, and revolutions, which had swept over Belgium, especially Flanders—and now He was taking it away. May His Holy Name be blessed!

CHAPTER 6

Flight

During dinner the bombardment had been at its height. In that short half-hour almost twenty shells had burst quite close to us. It was our side of the town that was being attacked—already a poor woman, begging for something to eat, had told the *portress* that the roof of the college was struck. Mother Prioress, deaf to all entreaties, said that everyone without exception was to be ready at 2 o'clock. We went about, looking—perhaps for the last time—at the dear old scenes, which we had thought to leave only when death should knock at our door.

We had already placed on every window of the convent a paper badge of the Sacred Heart, and lastly erected a niche outside one of the garret windows, in which we put the miraculous statue of Our Lady of the Angels, which had remained unhurt outside the monastery in the siege of Ypres, in 1744. We had done all we could and must now abandon all, leaving everything under the double protection of the Mother and the Son.

A little after 2 o'clock the hand-cart came round to the door. All the packages could not fit in it, in spite of Reverend Mother having made us take out nearly all we had gathered together; for she had learnt by experience, in carrying the things she had prepared for Lady Abbess as far as Vlamertinghe, three days before, the difficulties of walking so far, and carrying a heavy parcel at the same time. The enclosure door was then fastened on the inside, and all other important rooms or cupboards being likewise locked, we passed with a last farewell through the long-loved choir, which had known the joys and sorrows of our whole religious life.

We then went through the outer church into the sacristy, locking the door of the grille behind us. There was but one more door which separated us from the outside world—one door more! and we should be out of our enclosure, perhaps never more to return! There was a pause in our sad procession—the key was not there. Our Lord watched over us once more; for, had we then continued in our procession, some of us would inevitably have been badly hurt, if not indeed killed. After a few minutes' waiting, the key was brought, and already placed in the keyhole, when a loud explosion, accompanied by a terrific crash which shook the entire building, laid us all prostrate . . . Bewildered, rather than afraid, we arose, and saw, through the window, a shower of bricks and glass falling into the garden. The first—though not the last—shell had struck our well-loved abbey.

We now realised that there was no time to waste. Already Edmund was screaming out from the other side of the still-locked door. 'Why don't you come? I told you, you should have left long ago. The convent is struck! We shall all be killed if you don't make haste!' The door was opened, and with an indescribable feeling of horror, mingled with uncertainty, we went out. In the street we raised our eyes in one sad farewell to our beloved monastery; and there, out of the cell windows, principally that of Mother Prioress, a cloud of vapour and smoke told us of the passage of the shell; while the remains of the garret windows overhead and other debris of slates, bricks, wood and glass, strewn on the pavement, proved without a doubt, that Divine Providence had truly intervened in allowing the little delay in the sacristy, but for which we should have been just on the spot when all this had happened. A cry of anguish arose from our hearts as, hurrying along the deserted street, we saw our convent thus apparently burning.

Halfway down the street, another explosion behind us made us look round to see if the abbey had again been struck, but no! this time it was the Institut Saint-Louis, just in front. Turning the corner, we saw some 'Tommies' scrambling out of a house which had also been shelled. As we stumbled over the bricks which covered the road, Edmund hurrying us on for bare life, one of the soldiers caught sight of us, and calling out to another to come to help 'the Sisters' he threw down the bundle he was carrying, and seizing two of ours, he walked along with us, his comrade doing the same. We shall continue the narrative from the notes of Dame Patrick:—

As we were nearing the Rue de Lille, where the shells were falling thickly, two soldiers came forward to help us with our packages. We chatted as we hurried along, stopping every one or two minutes, to avoid a shower of bricks, as we heard a shell hiss over our heads and fall on one of the houses by us. One of us remarked to the soldiers: " It is very kind of you to help us." To our delight they answered, "It is our same religion, and our same country." They were both Irish Catholics—one from Kerry, the other from Belfast. When we reached the outskirts of the town they were both obliged to turn back, not having leave to quit Ypres. The Kerry man left us hurriedly; but our man from Belfast ventured a little farther, though in the end he thought it wiser to return to his regiment. So we shook hands with him, and thanked him heartily, wishing him good luck and a safe return to dear old Ireland! Our good Mother Prioress had a bag of pears in her hand, so she said to him: "Here, take these pears and eat them, and we will pray for you."

But he turned away, and said, "No, no, keep them for your-selves." Here the poor fellow broke down and cried. He hurried away, waved his hand, and wished us Godspeed. I happened, during this little scene, just to have moved on, thinking Mother Prioress was by me. However, on looking round, I saw she was some distance behind, so I walked back to join her. To my surprise, I found her weeping. I felt very shaky myself, but did not want to seem so. I jokingly said, "Oh! Mother Prioress, what is the matter?" Then she told me what had happened, and said, "I could keep up no longer when I saw that dear, kind, genuine Irish-hearted man break down—how I wish I could know his name!"

"Come along," I said, "let us hope that one day we shall find it out, but don't cry any more or you'll have me joining in too." I then thought on my brave, tender-hearted countrymen who had left home and country to serve in the British Army as Belgium's friends and protectors, and I felt proud and happy that we Irish Benedictines should have fallen in so often with Irishmen, always meeting with the same kind-heartedness . . .'

We had left the town in a terrible state. Through several streets which we passed, we could not see the other side on account of the clouds of smoke and dust, occasioned by the bursting of the shells and the falling buildings. Several telegraph posts lay across the road, with the wires hopelessly twisted and broken. Soldiers were running to and fro, propping up walls which had been shaken by an explosion in the vicinity, or making for some new ruin to see if they could be of any use. At last leaving the terrible sight behind us, we passed by the Rue d'Elverdinghe, on to the road leading to Poperinghe. Here we picked up the good fellow who was pushing the hand-cart. He took some more packages, tying them all together with a stout rope to prevent them falling off. His wife and little children were also there, for they dared not remain in the town. How glad were we now that Reverend Mother had listened to our chaplain, when he told her not to wait till the last moment to place dear Lady Abbess in safety. What would she have done in the midst of those dreadful shells, which, although we had left the town far behind us, still continued—though we heard them not so loudly now—to fly on their errand of destruction towards poor, unfortunate Ypres.

There is no need to describe the marching of the troops as they passed us on the way, as Mother Prioress has already mentioned it in her notes. What left the deepest impression on our memories was the thick slimy mire we had to wade through. In some places it was so bad that it was almost impossible to get on—we seemed to slide back two steps for every one that we made forward. We trudged bravely on, but before we had gone a quarter of the way some of us were already *au bout*. We, who for years had not walked more than six or seven times round our little garden, were certainly little fitted to go some nine miles in that dreadful mud, and carrying parcels which, by this time, seemed to weigh tons. At last Vlamertinghe came in sight. If only it had been Poperinghe! We were not even quite halfway. We could hardly push through the crowds of fugitives, each with his or her bundles of different colour, shape, and size.

Some men had four packages, two in front and two behind, slung over their shoulders; others were bent in two with huge sacks on their backs; others pushed wheelbarrows or perambulators in front of them; while some were content with a little bundle tied up in a pocket-handkerchief. One respectable-looking man carefully hugged two umbrellas—were they his only treasures? We passed through the village, and on, on, on! always in company of troops, motorcars, and refugees. The latter accosted us from time to time to ask who we were and where we came from. They nearly all seemed to know the Iersche Van Damen von S. Jacob's Straat! Several officers and soldiers saluted us also as we passed. If only the driver of some motorcar would have given us a lift, but they flew past so quickly—they probably did not even see us.

The mason's little children took turn by turn to have a ride on the hand-cart, seated on the top of all the bundles, while the others hung out of the poor mother's arms, who cheered them on, and told them wonderful tales in Flemish. One little boy was squeezing an almost imperceptible black puppy, which he would not let go for all the world. While the young gentleman was having his turn for a ride there was a sudden halt on the way. The wee doggie had managed to wriggle out of his master's tight embrace and, making good use of his long-sighed-for liberty, had fallen out of the cart. Luckily, no bones were broken, owing to the soft carpet of mud into which he sank. Indeed, the poor cart was obliged to stop more than once, either to make way for two regiments who were marching in different directions, or for two or three motorcars passing all at once, and, often enough, getting literally 'stuck in the mud,' or to give a rest to Edmund and the workman, who had a hard time of it.

It was now getting dark, and a thick mist was rising. The sound of the firing was getting more and more feeble as we left Ypres farther and farther behind. From time to time, a dead horse, stretched out in the ditch or in a field close by, would make us turn away from the mournful sight. We walked and walked—would we never arrive at our destination? It became darker at every moment—we were obliged to keep well together, for fear of being left' behind. The trees which lined the road loomed out as though they had been some unearthly spectres, with their leafless branches like gaunt arms uplifted towards the sky to call down vengeance on the earth; while, magnified through the thick mist, the moon tinged with red seemed to reflect the bloodshed and carnage of the battle-field.

At last we caught sight of a feeble glimmer which—unlike the lights of the motorcars, as they sped along, throwing an electric flash into our dazzled eyes and then vanishing, leaving the darkness more intense—grew brighter and brighter as we advanced. Could it really be Poperinghe? We hastened on, almost forgetting our fatigue. Yes, we were truly there—it was Poperinghe! But where were we to turn our steps? Soon we were surrounded by a crowd. Soldiers and civilians, men and women, looked with commiseration on this new group of fugitives who added to the number of those who already filled the town. Reverend Mother asked to be directed to the Carmelites, remembering the recommendation of Mr. Tack. Two girls offered to conduct us there. At this moment a gentleman came forward asking what we desired (we only discovered later that it was the Judge).

In a few words, Mother Prioress explained the situation. On hearing mention made of La Sainte Union, where Lady Abbess had taken refuge, he informed us it was quite close at hand, that if we wished he would conduct us there first; and in case there should not be room for us all, he would undertake to find us lodgings. Needless to say, we willingly accepted the proposal, and in a few minutes we found ourselves in a cheery little parlour, awaiting the Superioress' decision. The permission was accorded at first rather hesitatingly, and for one night only. Was it astonishing? The poor nuns had just given up the school premises to the French Ambulance; they had also given refuge to a community from Oostnienukerke, who were afterwards rejoined by their sisters from Passchendaele, and now we arrived also!

However, when they discovered that we really were what we made ourselves out to be, and not German spies, or vagrants—and especially as, during the conversation, one of the elder nuns found that she had formerly been the mistress of Mother Prioress when she had been to the convent at Hazebrouck in preparation for her first Communion, the community having been expelled from France eleven years before—they soon changed, and for a whole fortnight showed us every kind of hospitality.

Now Dame Placid and Sister Romana heard the news, and came running down to welcome us, then Sister Magdalen and dear Dame Josephine. The meeting was a happy one, which however soon changed to sadness, when we related what had happened to the old Abbey. We were impatient to see our beloved Lady Abbess. Soon our dear prioress, who had gone first to break the news gently, reappeared, and we all trooped upstairs, little dreaming of the sad scene which that very little parlour would witness in less than a fortnight's time. Lady Abbess was at once both anxious and pleased; so, after an exchange of greetings, and having received her blessing, we retired. We now began to realise what we had done. It was all so strange; we were now truly poor, not knowing what would befall us. '*Sacré Coeur de Jésus, j'ai confiance en Vous!*' We were really and truly destitute of all human aid, and depended solely on our loving Father in Heaven for everything.

Soon the good nuns had prepared supper for us, after which we made a visit to the church, and then were not sorry to be shown the way to the dormitory. It had belonged to the children, who, owing to the war, had not returned after the holidays. Oh dear! "Where were our cells? Here there were not even alcoves, but some pretty-looking curtains covering two sides of each bed. We were not even alone in the dormitory, several beds being already occupied. Suddenly, to our great surprise, Antoinette Doone, one of our old pupils, who had always remained especially attached to Mother Prioress, threw herself into Reverend Mother's arms saying that she also was stopping at La Sainte Union with her two servants. She was delighted at the idea of sharing the dormitory with her old mistresses. Truly the war brought about strange coincidences, and made us meet with devoted friends when we least expected it. Soon we were reposing on a soft mattress and spring bed, and unaccustomed to such luxury, as well as worn out by the fatigues of the day, we were not long in falling asleep.

CHAPTER 7

Visiting the Wounded

It was late the next morning when we awoke, for there were no guns to disturb our slumbers. However, we were up in time for the last Mass. Having breakfasted, we set to work to carry our parcels upstairs, and to clean our shoes, which, owing to our peregrinations, were hardly recognisable, being simply clotted with mire and dirt. This finished, we made our first visit to the wounded soldiers in the ambulance. What a scene of suffering met our eyes! If it made us realise, more than ever, that we had left our beloved enclosure, still it gave us an insight into human misery which we should never have had, had we remained peacefully in our abbey. The *ensemble* was not yet organised, only those downstairs having bedsteads—the poor soldiers upstairs lying on straw on the floor. The impression made was ineffaceable. We now saw what war really meant, and we left, after having distributed little cakes, biscuits and sweets, with a promise to come back as often as we could.

Mother Prioress was now called for, to see Edmund and the poor family who had not been received in the convent, as the Superioress had been threatened with a summons if she received any refugees. They had been directed to the police station, where, having presented themselves, they had been placed in an inn, and had passed the night in an attic on some straw. They were also starving, having had nothing to eat. They were quickly given some of our provisions, and Mother Prioress paid the mason for his hard work of the day before. Being now a little consoled, he said he would go off with his wife and children to a village close by, to see if he would not be more successful in getting a lodging there. Edmund remained, lamenting loudly over his misfortunes. The chaplain of the community passing by, and hearing his sad tale, had compassion on the poor man, and told him he might sleep at his house, while the nuns arranged to give him his meals. After some days, however, he found the priest's house too far away from the convent, and so managed to get a bed in a baker's establishment just opposite.

Every morning we had the happiness of assisting at two or four Masses; for besides the director of the community, whose Mass Edmund served, some French priests who were attached to the ambulance also requested permission to celebrate the Holy Sacrifice. Reverend Mother arranged with the Superioress that we might go to the chapel when we liked to say our office, where—instead of stalls—turning the chairs to face each other, we improvised a choir, and recited the Benedictine hours with the usual ceremonies. We were, of course, obliged to advance the night office, saying *vespers* and *compline* at 2.30 and *matins* and *lauds* at 4.0, it being often necessary to bring the chairs close to the window to have light to finish, if, as it sometimes happened, we were unable to keep to the given hours.

On Sunday afternoon, eleven nuns from the Rue de Lille at Ypres came to beg a themselves since the outbreak of the war in our parts to tending the wounded soldiers. It was they who had had such a narrow escape when the Germans came to Ypres, whilst they had their convent full of Belgians. They told us afterwards how good their wounded had been, and how the greater part, as soon as they were well enough, used to come to Benediction and sing with the nuns.

Now, however, they brought sad news from the town, which was being bombarded worse than ever. They had been obliged to fly for their lives; one sister had been killed by a bomb, a servant badly wounded, and their Superioress had stopped behind with two nuns, compelling the others to leave. They had at first taken the wrong road, going straight to the scene of battle; but being sent back by the British soldiers, they had made their way, as best they could, to Poperinghe. They had lost six of their number, not knowing what had become of them; seventeen had left the convent, and now only eleven had arrived at Poperinghe.

The next day our servant-man came round to say that he had received an invitation to go back to Ypres the following day with another man, who was willing to run the risk of returning. Needless to say we were delighted to have such a good chance of getting news about our monastery; and all prayed for his safety. We anxiously awaited the result of this venture, hoping that he would be able to get into the convent, and that, above all, no harm would happen to him.

True enough, he came back in triumph, dragging another huge parcel of things he had managed to secure for himself. The dreadful account he gave of the monastery filled us with despair, for, according to his description, half the building seemed to have been destroyed. Happily, the person who had accompanied him called the next day, and told us that Edmund had greatly exaggerated the mischief done; and he hoped that if the Germans could be repulsed, we should be able to return in four or five days.

Mother Prioress determined to ascertain the truth of the case for herself. She accordingly made enquiries as to whether it would be possible to go to Ypres in a motorcar. M. Vander Meersch, a solicitor who lived near the abbey, came to our help, and an officer was found who was willing to take two nuns with him. We begged our dear prioress not to expose herself to such evident danger; but, as usual, she would not listen, and it was decided that Dame Placid should accompany her. God, Who ever protects those who put their trust in Him, arranged otherwise, and the motorcar was prevented from leaving Poperinghe. We heard afterwards that at the very time that they should have arrived, a bomb had fallen on another motor, and killed five officers.

During the next days, news poured in from Ypres. At one time, we heard that the Germans had been repulsed, and their guns captured, and that Ypres would soon be quite safe again; shortly afterwards, it was announced that the enemy was mercilessly bombarding the town, some houses were falling, others burning. We were more than ever convinced that we could believe nothing that we heard and must necessarily see for ourselves. Besides, the guns which we had only heard feebly in the distance, on our arrival at Poperinghe, could certainly be heard far more distinctly now; were we going to be bombarded a second time? It really seemed probable, for German aeroplanes appeared in sight, apparently scrutinising the movements of the Allies, and had not that been the beginning of the hostilities at Ypres?

In the streets, the regiments passed and repassed—the poor, brave fellows marching off to the battle, and the others coming back from the trenches to have a well-merited repose. It was often touching to see how those who had not been ordered out would await the return of the troops, anxiously scanning the lines as they passed, and on perceiving a comrade, perhaps a 'chum,' coming back unhurt, they would run forward and give a hand-shake with a joyful greeting, as the horses trotted by. But alas! there were always a number of empty saddles, belonging to those who had been taken to the ambulance, or—worse still—left dead on the battlefield. The horses themselves seemed mournful, as they followed mechanically after the others, as though they felt it must be partially their fault that their dear masters were no longer there. Often, also, numbers of German prisoners would march past between two files of British or French soldiers on their way to the station.

Our poor wounded French soldiers were not forgotten. By this time things were arranged better; nearly all had beds now, some even sheets. And this was due to the unflagging devotion of three priests attached to the ambulance as *infirmarians*. They certainly preached to us a silent sermon of self-forgetfulness and heroic charity; and our greatest pleasure was to hear them relate all they had gone through since the war broke out. In the French Army alone, 40,000 priests mixed with the common soldiers, the greater number being combatants. The brave wounded also gave us many a lesson, never finding fault with anything, never complaining of their dreadful wounds. And yet how horribly some of them were mutilated! A great number were obliged to have an arm or leg amputated—one had his lower jaw carried away—another, his whole face from below the eyes. Most of them were wounded in the head, which made them suffer dreadfully, some even being delirious.

There were some who belonged to the highest aristocracy—counts and barons were there, lying on straw or hard stretchers; others again were quite young, only twenty or twenty-one. Yet all were patient, all courageous, all sure that in the end the Allies would win, and the Germans be defeated. The unfortunate victims who died of their wounds were carried out to a little hut or tent erected in the garden. As we passed by, we would lift up the curtain which hid them from view, and say a '*De profundis*' for the repose of their souls. Sometimes as many as eleven or twelve lay there, awaiting the coffins which could not be made quickly enough. One poor *Zouave*, who had probably been dead some time before it was found out, lay there with his arms uplifted, as though he still held the gun, with which he would, even in death, lay low his enemy.

But we cannot do better than take from the notes of Dame Teresa, who was so devoted in visiting the ambulance:—

At Poperinghe we spent all our time making badges of the Sacred Heart for the wounded soldiers. Almost every day we went to visit them. This gave us the greatest joy. The first time we entered the large room No. 1, where they lay, some on beds, others on stretchers, we were struck with horror and pity. There they were, young men and middle-aged, from every department of France; some had been struck on the head, others on the chest, back, or shoulders, or else wounded in the legs. And yet not one complaint escaped their lips—only one poor fellow, who was delirious, called out as we passed by: "My head, my head! oh, if you only knew what it is to have such a headache." Another soldier, just twenty-one, said to us in the patois of the South of France, "*Franche! Franche!* shall I ever see thee again!" We went from one room to another, speaking to each, and cheering them up. We gave them pears, and it used to be our greatest pleasure to peel them, cut them in small bits, and now and again we would put them in their mouths, when they were unable to move. They were as simple as children, and loved our visits. "Sister, you'll come back tomorrow won't you? It is so nice to see you, it cheers us up!"

I remember one incident, which shows their simplicity. Dame Walburge and I had been going round, distributing small bits of pear, which they much relished as very comforting to their parched lips; but there came a time when we had exhausted our last pear, and still many soldiers had not had a bit. Of course next day we would serve them the first; but Dame Walburge whispered to tell me one poor fellow had been watching me so anxiously for some time. I turned towards him to say a little word of comfort, but he interrupted me, saying in a fretful, childish way: "Oh, Sister, and you have given me no pear, and I wanted one so badly!" In vain we searched our pockets, all the while promising he should be served the first next day. He repeated: "It's tonight I wanted it." We left the room sadly, wishing, for once in our religious lives, that we had a penny to buy him a pear. But Almighty God, Who is all-powerful, heard the prayer of His children; for hardly had I told this story to one of the nuns of La Sainte Union, than she gave me a pear, and though it was already dark, we ran back joyfully to our poor wounded soldier, who seemed dumb for joy, but his happy face rewarded us beyond words.

The unselfishness of the soldiers towards each other was marvellous; once, while peeling a pear for a soldier—one who was eating a piece of bread—he said to me: "Sister, I am sure my neighbour would also like a piece." I turned to the other, who answered timidly: "Yes, I should like it; but see, Sister, I have a little bit of meat on my bread, and he has none, so give it to him!" Needless to say, I divided it between them.

'Sometimes they would give us a little money out of their purses to buy biscuits, or cheese, or, as they said, "something to eat." One *Zouave* asked us to buy him a pair of socks.

At this French Ambulance we also had the joy of making the acquaintance of three soldier-priests, who daily said Mass at the convent, thus giving us the happiness of sometimes hearing five Masses a day. I do not quite remember the names of the priests. I think one was called M. l'Abbé Tecq, another M. l'Abbé Couq of Dijon, and the third was M. l'Abbé Louis Charbonnel of Avignon. This latter was very fond of Benedictines, and gave us a special blessing before leaving, assuring us that we should immediately feel "at home" among our sisters at Oulton.

These priests were more than devoted to the soldiers, administering the last sacraments, and bringing Holy Communion to them, no matter at what time of the day. The little badges of the Sacred Heart also did their work; all the soldiers asked to have them, and insisted on our pinning them ourselves on their clothes; the priests wore them, and distributed hundreds, so that we could scarcely keep pace with their fervour, except by working at them every free minute we had. Some of the *infirmarians* even asked to have a few to send away in their letters.

They wrought many conversions—the soldiers all wanted to have them.'

Again there was dreadful news from Ypres. The hospital was entirely destroyed. The British soldiers had gone with their motorcars to take away the four nuns, who still risked their lives by staying to tend the poor victims, who were daily struck down in or about the town. Four other nuns had been killed in their cellar. A priest carrying the holy oils to a dying person had been struck down in the street. The Germans had even made new bombs, bigger and more destructive than those used before. What should we do? Would it not be wiser to accept Lady Abbess of Oulton's kind invitation, and go straight on to England while there was yet time? But our abbey! Why leave it, if we could possibly return?

We found ourselves surrounded at Poperinghe by every attention which charity could suggest; and although the community of La Sainte Union had often the greatest difficulty to provide for the increased number of fugitives, there being two other communities as well as ourselves, still we received everything that was possible in the circumstances. However, as the officer in charge of the ambulance demanded one thing after another for his soldiers, he came at last to claim the room which had been placed at our disposal. The Superioress was obliged to yield, and the 'chef' soon established the supplies of food in what had been our refectory. We were now forced to take possession of the nuns' refectory, going to our meals before or after theirs.

We thus found ourselves at table not only with the two other communities above mentioned, but also with the servants of one of our old pupils, who were also stopping in the convent to help at the ambulance. We managed as best we could, and still kept up our tradition of entering in procession, saying the '*De profundis*,' and then reciting the Benedictine grace before and after meals. This was not all. There was a door at one end, which led into the room given up to the soldiers; consequently, at any moment, one would appear in the refectory to fetch a loaf of bread, or some meat, &c., and then repass again on his way out. Once, when a priest came, Mother Prioress gave him a pear, as also to the soldier who came after him; but soon the Superioress put up a large screen, which enabled them to enter without disturbing the community. They had a very hard life. Often we saw their shadows through the mat glass as they stood at the windows, eating their dinners in the rain and snow.

And now Our Lord was preparing a cross which we had not counted on, and which added to the grief that already weighed down our hearts. Our poor dear Dame Josephine, already fifty-two years professed, now left us. Feeble and infirm, the shock had been too much for her. The want of good nourishment had also told on her—she was soon obliged to keep her bed, having caught cold. The doctor, on seeing her, declared the case dangerous, and proposed that she should receive the last sacraments. This took place on Friday, November 13, Feast of all the Saints of the Benedictine Order. Alas! we little expected that another one would so soon increase their happy company. Saturday, our dear patient seemed to rally a little, and none of us believed the *infirmarian*, when, in the evening, she told us she was dying.

However, Mother Prioress remained some time alone with Dame

Josephine, helping her to renew her vows, and offer up holy aspirations. She herself did not think she was so bad; but, always ready to obey, she followed the prayers suggested by her whom she had known when she had been Sister Maura—a lively, fervent, eighteen-year-old postulant, and whom she had always cared for as a mother. Now that her dearly-loved little novice had grown into her Superioress, she submitted herself with childlike simplicity, asking her blessing morning and evening, thus edifying greatly the whole community. She therefore now made, when Dame Maura proposed it, her act of resignation, should God demand the sacrifice of her life.

Two of us offered to divide the night between us to watch by her bedside. After 1 a.m. she slept a little, though her breathing was difficult. At 2.30 she awoke, and seemed rather restless. Before going down in the morning, Mother Prioress paid Dame Josephine another visit; but we could no longer distinguish what she said. We replaced each other during the Masses; but about 7.30 everyone was called out of church, there being now no more doubt. The Superioress of the house knelt with Mother Prioress close by the bed, and several nuns of both communities joined their prayers to ours, during which our dearest jubilarian breathed forth her innocent soul.

It was the Feast of the Dedication of the Churches. Our Lord had chosen the day Himself, for had she not passed her whole religious life in the service of the altar as *sacristine?* And by a curious coincidence, in which we may again detect the loving attention of the Divine Master, the burial, settled at first for Tuesday, was put off till Wednesday, Feast of the Dedication of Saint Peter and Saint Paul. Sad at any time, the loss of our dear Dame Josephine now appeared doubly so—in exile, and in the midst of so many other trials. She had truly 'chosen the better part,' and we felt a sort of relief to know that she had been spared the horrors which we should, in all probability, live to see. Everyone showed us the kindest sympathy in our loss. Dame Aloysius and Dame Columban performed the last duties to the dear departed one, and laid her out in the same little parlour where she had come to welcome us, just nine days before, on the evening of our arrival.

Everyone came to pray by her corpse, all the nuns, the chaplain, even several of our old pupils, who, having taken refuge in Poperinghe, heard of our sad loss—and last of all, poor old Edmund who for a moment forgot his own troubles to grieve over dear Dame Josephine whom, like everyone else, he had esteemed and respected. Each, as they left the little room, where such a peaceful silence reigned, declared they had never before seen such a holy and happy death.

Thanks to the intervention of M. Vander Meersch, already mentioned, and who was a personal friend of the *burgomaster* of Poperinghe, Mother Prioress obtained permission to place the dead body, having previously secured it in a double coffin, in a private vault in the cemetery; so that if—which God grant—we are able to rebuild our monastery at Ypres, we shall then lay dear Dame Josephine with her other religious sisters.

We recited the Office of the Dead round the holy remains, in the convent chapel, and sang the *Requiem* Mass at the funeral. This latter should have really taken place in the parish church, but the *curé*, kindly sympathising with our numerous trials, offered to perform it at the convent so that we should be thus enabled to keep our enclosure as much as possible. We sang the Mass (at which all attended) with great devotion, in spite of the severe colds we had all caught. At the moment of consecration, when, in deepest recollection, we adored 'Our Lord and our God,' Who thus deigned to come down from Heaven among His sorrowing children, the well-known hiss of a descending bomb made itself heard, and in the same moment a formidable explosion took place quite close to us.

The Holy Sacrifice continued without interruption. It was only afterwards we heard that the Germans had aimed at the ambulance established, as has been said, in La Sainte Union. Missing us by a few yards only, the bomb had struck the house next door, doing, however, but little damage. Four girls of the Congregation of Our Blessed Lady carried the coffin to the cemetery, while the nuns of the house accompanied our community. The sad little procession wound its way along the muddy streets, amidst troops of civilians and soldiers. Nearly all saluted as it passed. The prayers being sung at the grave, the coffin was deposited in the vault, and we returned silently, stopping to recite '*De profundis*' at the little portion of ground allotted to the dead nuns of La Sainte Union.

CHAPTER 8

An Attempt to Revisit Ypres

When we arrived at the convent, we found that a soldier had called
to say that a motorcar would be starting for Ypres at 4.30, but which
would not return until the next day. We felt hardly inclined to accept the invitation, but dared not miss the opportunity which would
perhaps not present itself a second time. Mother Prioress and Dame
Placid decided to go, and to pass the night in the abbey and come
back the following day in the motor. We were all so anxious at the
idea that two of us, *viz*. Dame Columban and Dame Patrick, offered
to go on foot to be able to help in case of danger. The narrative will be
continued from the notes of Dame Columban and Dame Patrick:—

We set off at 2.30 as we should, of course, take longer than
the motor. Two of the servants of Madame Boone, who were
also in the convent, accompanied us, to be able to see in what
state her house was. At their suggestion we decided to follow
the railway line, instead of going by the high road; and thus we
were spared the dreadful mud and constant traffic we should
otherwise have had. On our way we met many poor people
who were flying from Ypres; for the Germans were still shelling
it. They tried their best to dissuade us from our purpose, depict-
ing in vivid colours the great danger we were incurring—we,
however, continued on our way. Several aeroplanes passed overhead, one of which received a volley of shots, so we knew it
must have been an enemy. Sad to say, it escaped untouched.

As we advanced we heard the sound of the guns louder and
louder, till at last we found ourselves once again in the noise
and confusion we had left a week and a half ago. Our hearts
beat faster as we began to distinguish in the distance the tower

of St. Martin's and of the Hall; and we hastened our steps, wondering if the motorcar, which was to bring Mother Prioress and Dame Placid, were already there, and making plans as to what we should do for the night. The fugitives had told us that the Germans were principally shelling the station, so we determined to go round the town, and come in by the Porte de Menin which would bring us immediately to the abbey. As we were thus settling everything in advance, we came to where the railway lines pass over the high road, and were about to continue by the latter, when a French policeman suddenly stopped us, asking where we were going.

We bravely replied, "To Ypres!" What was our dismay when he politely informed us he was forbidden to allow anyone to enter the town. In vain we expostulated, saying how far we had come, that we only desired to see our monastery once again, that it was quite impossible to walk back to Poperinghe that night. It was all useless. As we spoke, some poor persons endeavoured also to pass, but were sent back. We then asked the officer if he had seen a motor-car with two nuns in it. He replied in the negative, but promised to stop them should they pass. He tried to mend matters by explaining that he was obliged to obey orders, and that it was to prevent deserted houses being broken into and robbed that persons were not allowed to enter the town. "For," he said, "people pass by empty-handed in the morning, saying they want to see if their houses are still standing; they come back in the evening loaded with things; is it their own belongings they have, or someone else's?" This, however, did not console us, and we turned our steps disconsolately towards Poperinghe.

It was nearly six o'clock. The cold wind beat pitilessly in our faces, for it was freezing hard. The stars were shining, but there was no moon, so the road was dark. Should we ever reach Poperinghe again? What if Mother Prioress and Dame Placid were waiting for us at the abbey? They would assuredly think we were killed! , . . We walked slowly on, debating what was to be done. At last we decided to try to find a lodging for the night, and get into Ypres the first thing in the morning. We stopped at the first group of houses which came in sight. What was our joy to see a motor outside. Perhaps we could get a ride home. We addressed ourselves to the French soldier who was standing by, and asked if by chance he was going to Poperinghe that night. "Yes!" was the rather laconic reply.

"And would it be possible to take us also?" That was another thing. We must wait for the officer, who would be back, perhaps, in half an hour, perhaps later. Then, as if to excuse his apparent unwillingness, the soldier told us they were strictly forbidden, under pain of thirty days' imprisonment, to take anyone in the motors, as it had been discovered that German spies had been acting as chauffeurs to several French officers. Did we look like German spies? Be that as it may, it was not inviting to think of waiting in the cold for half an hour or more, and then meeting with a probable refusal. We consequently returned to our first idea of getting a night's lodging.

We knocked at the first door, but found the house full of French soldiers. We went farther on, and, through a window, saw some English "Tommies" seated round the fire with the members of the family. This looked more inviting. We pushed the door open (there being no sign of a bell or knocker), and at our enquiry, were told that the house was full, there being four officers lodging there, as well as the private soldiers. We asked if it would be possible to speak to an officer, and were requested to step inside.

Our visit being announced, a cheery voice called out, "*Entrez, mes Soeurs, entrez!*" We entered the little room, and found ourselves in presence of four officers, who were actually engaged in making their tea, and who were more than delighted on learning our nationality. They were very interested in our story, and pressed us to take tea with them. We thanked them for their kindness, but refused, not wishing to deprive them of what they so well deserved. Two of them next offered to go in search of some means of conveying us back to Poperinghe, as we were not likely to find a lodging anywhere. They were also sure that the officer had never left with Mother Prioress, for—as one of them remarked—"Ypres is a very unhealthy place for the moment." After some time, the two returned, saying they had found a French vehicle, which would conduct us to within a mile of Poperinghe. So, thanking our kind hosts, we followed our two guides to the place where the carriage (if so we may call it, it being rather a closed cart, drawn by mules) was standing. The soldiers were busy unloading it.

As we were talking, two lights appeared in the distance, which rapidly grew bigger and brighter, as a motorcar dashed past us. The two officers soon chased it, calling on the driver to stop. He accordingly slowed down, and we learned, to our great delight, that the officer (an English one this time) would take us straight to Poperinghe. We were soon spinning along the road, leaving Vlamertinghe, houses, carts, horses, soldiers, far behind us; and in a good quarter of an hour, we stopped at the door of La Sainte Union. We begged our kind benefactor to accept something for our drive; but he refused, saying he was only too pleased to have been able to render us this little service. As soon as we were safe inside, we were surrounded, all asking what had happened to us, for everyone had been more than anxious on our account, owing to the alarming news which was brought from Ypres. We related our adventures in a few words, and then had to go quickly upstairs to show ourselves to dear Lady Abbess, who was greatly troubled over our absence, and enquired constantly if we had yet arrived.

In our turn we now desired to know what had happened to Mother Prioress and Dame Placid, so, during recreation, which we shared with the other nuns, refugees like ourselves, we heard of their doings. After going out in search of the officer who was to take them to Ypres, and waiting in the rain and cold, the soldier who had called in the morning found them and said the captain had been delayed, and would not leave before 4 or 4.30. They had then returned to the convent and set out once again, this time taking the key of the abbey, which they had previously forgotten.

Arrived in the market square, they saw a long row of motors drawn up, with soldiers busy taking off the cakes of mud and mire which literally covered them. In vain they looked for their driver. At this moment a regiment of *Chasseurs Français* rode up four abreast. They had hardly gone when the dragoons, with their uniform of pale blue and silver, galloped past also. This state of things lasted almost an hour. The captain not yet making any appearance, they had gone in quest of something to take with them to eat, in case no food should be found in Ypres.

By a strange coincidence, on entering the shop, they were accosted by the manageress of one of the hotels of Ypres, who immediately recognised them. At last, on coming once more out into the square, the soldier met them again, saying that the bombardment was raging so fiercely that there was no question of leaving Poperinghe that afternoon. It was useless to think of sending after us, so everyone had remained in the greatest anxiety until our return.

CHAPTER 9

Preparing to Start for England

Reverend Mother, despairing of getting into Ypres, was now determined to leave Poperinghe and go to England; but again the question presented itself—How were we to get there? As the English officers had been so kind to us in our efforts to get to Ypres on the previous evening, she thought that perhaps they would help us also for the journey. Dame Teresa offered to accompany her, as, being the niece of Mr. Redmond, it was felt she might be specially useful. So, accompanied by Dame Columban and Dame Patrick, Mother Prioress set out to try to find the officer who had given them seats in his motor the day before. He had said he belonged to the aeroplane encampment, which we knew to be just outside the town. Meeting an English soldier, we asked him to be so kind as to show us the way.

On hearing our story, he advised us to apply rather to another officer, who would be better able to help us, and directed us to the convent where this officer was staying. The convent proved to be that of the Penitents of St. Francis, where we received a warm welcome, and were introduced to two nuns from the Hospice of Ypres who had taken refuge there. The captain in question was not in; so the nuns insisted on our seeing their lovely little church and sacristy, after which they found a soldier who conducted us to the British Headquarters which were then actually at Poperinghe. There we were received with the greatest courtesy by Captain Liddell who promised to do everything in his power to help us, but advised us, at the same time, to apply to Commandant Delporte, of the Belgian Constabulary, who would be better able than he to find a train to convey us to Dunkerque or Boulogne.

We thanked the captain, and left to find the Belgian police station. Having been directed several different ways, we eventually arrived at our destination, and were received by an official who promised to acquaint the *commandant* with the reason of our visit as soon as he should return, he being absent at the moment. We were about to leave, when the door opened and M. le Commandant Delporte entered, and after courteously saluting us, he begged us to take seats, and showed the greatest interest in all that Mother Prioress related. He then said that a train of refugees had left only the day before, and he could not tell us when another would start. He referred us again to the general staff, saying that, as we were British subjects, they ought certainly to take us either in their ambulance cars or in a train for the wounded on account of Our Lady Abbess who was paralysed, adding that he would speak in our favour.

We therefore turned our steps once more to where we had come from, and having made known the result of our visit, we were told to return the next day at 1.30 p.m., before which time Captain Liddell would consult the chief medical officer, and see what could be done for us. We then took the road back to the convent, where we were glad to find a warm shelter.

The next day was Friday. Captain Liddell had promised to call on us, should anything be decided before 1.30. The town was, however, suddenly thrown into a state of excitement by the passing of a German Taube which dropped a bomb on St. Bertin's Church. Fortunately it only slightly injured the porch, though it wounded several persons standing by. Amongst the injured was the chaplain of La Sainte Union, whose hand was hurt. We were next informed that the British Head-quarters had left the town. What then would become of the arrangements for our journey to England? Immediately Dame Columban and Dame Patrick offered to go and see if any message had been left for us, poor Mother Prioress being unwell, and therefore not able to go herself. The narrative is again continued from the notes of Dame Columban and Dame Patrick:—

Having received Mother Prioress' blessing, we started off, wondering what we should find, perhaps an empty house? On our way we passed St. Bertin's Church, where a group of persons were gathered, watching French soldiers clearing the road of the remains of bricks, stones, glass, which were strewn about. Every window in the whole street was broken. Hastening our steps we were soon in presence of Captain Liddell, to whom we apologised for our early call, relating what we had heard. He said that the staff had no intention of leaving as yet, that as to our journey it would take several days to arrange, for different persons would have to be consulted. The situation did not seem very satisfactory, so, on taking our leave, we determined to have recourse once more to the Belgian authorities. Just as we arrived in sight of the building, to our great disappointment, we saw the *commandant* leaving in company with two British officers. We immediately drew back, but, recognising us, he came forward, all three officers giving a military salute.

We begged him not to stop for us, saying that we would call again, but he insisted on bringing us into the house, telling the officers he would rejoin them shortly. We stated, as briefly as possible, the unsatisfactory result of our visit to the English Headquarters, and asked what was the best thing to do. He told us that there was a train leaving the next day at 2.30 p.m., but that in all probability we should not enjoy the company. We, of course, declared that this did not matter. However, he told us to decide nothing as yet, saying he himself would go to arrange with the British officers, and would call on Mother Prioress next morning. We thanked him profusely, and once more turned our steps towards La Sainte Union to acquaint Reverend Mother with the result of our negotiations.

CHAPTER 10

A Second Attempt to Revisit Ypres

Were we, then, to leave Belgium without seeing our beloved monastery again? The thought was too dreadful. This time Dame Placid begged to be allowed to venture back, and asked Dame Columban and Dame Patrick if they would go with her. They at once agreed; and having begged a blessing from Mother Prioress, started off, accompanied by the two servants of Madame Boone, poor Mother Prioress being still unwell and quite unable to accompany them, to her great disappointment. Dame Columban and Dame Patrick will again tell the story.

We were now *determined* to succeed—it was our last chance.

We had not gone far, when the whirr of an aeroplane was heard overhead. It flew too low to be an enemy, so we wished it good-speed, and passed on. Shortly after, some fugitives met us, who, seeing the direction we were taking, stared aghast, and told us that the Germans were bombarding Ypres worse than ever. Should we turn back? Oh no! it was our *last* chance. We continued bravely. Soon, others stopped us with the same story, but, turning a deaf ear to the horrors they related, we pushed on. Over an hour had passed, when, after a brisk walk, Vlamertinghe came in sight. More than half our journey was accomplished. Just as we approached the railway station (we had again taken the railway track) we heard the whirr of an aeroplane, then a volley of shots flew up towards the aeroplane.

We knew what that meant. We could see the shots of the Allies bursting in the air, some near the Taube, some far away; alas! none hit it. What should we do? We determined to risk it; and passing under Taube, bombs, shots, and all, we hastened through the railway station—soldiers, men, women and children staring at "these strange Benedictine nuns!"

Hurrying on, we met two priests coming from Ypres. We stopped to ask advice. They told us that our undertaking was decidedly dangerous. There was hardly a person left in the town; they had gone in in the morning to see if they could be of any use, and were now leaving, not daring to stop the night. They told us that there was still one priest who remained in the establishment of the mad people, just outside Ypres, and that we could always call on him, if we could not manage to reach our convent; but they added that he also was leaving the next day with all his poor *protégés*. We made up our minds to risk all; so, asking the priests' blessing, we went our way. Other people tried in vain to make us turn back, especially two men who assured us we should never be able to accomplish our project.

We thanked them for the interest they showed in our behalf, and asked them if they would be so kind as to call at the convent at Poperinghe and tell Mother Prioress not to be anxious if we did not return that night, and not to expect us till the next day. We were now approaching the crossroads which had proved so fatal on Wednesday. A Belgian officer on a bicycle stopped to ask where we were going. We told him. He said it was simple madness to think of doing such a thing. He had been with his soldiers trying to mend the roads a little farther on, and had been obliged to leave off on account of the shells which were flying in all directions. We thanked him, but said we would risk it all the same.

Arriving on the high road, we soon found ourselves in presence of a French policeman who asked where we were going. "To Ypres!" was the determined reply. "No one can pass. You must go back." What were we to do? We determined to go on. Were there no means of getting in by another way? While we stood as though rooted to the ground, we caught sight of a French *chasseur* on the other side of the road, who seemed to have some authority, and who was trying to console a woman and two weeping children. We immediately applied to him, and told him our distress. He answered kindly, but told us, all the same, that he was afraid we should not be able to enter Ypres. We begged to be allowed to continue, if only to *try*. He smiled and said: "If you *really* wish it, then pass on." And on his writing

D. Teresa.   D. Placid.   D. Columban.   D. Patrick.

Mother Prioress.

THE MOTHER PRIORESS, DAME TERESA AND THE THREE NUNS WHO
REVISITED YPRES

down a passport, we went on triumphantly. It seemed as though God were helping us.

We had been so taken up with all that had passed that we had thought of nothing else, but now that we were in sight of the goal we realised that it was freezing hard. The stars were shining brightly, from time to time a light flashed in the distance, then a sinister whirr, followed by an explosion, which told us that the Germans were not going to let us pass as easily as did the French *chasseur*. Wondering as to how we should succeed, we came across an English sentinel, and so asked his advice. He told us that he thought there was no chance whatever of our getting into the town. He said that he himself had been obliged to abandon his post on account of the shells, that the troops in the town had been ordered to leave, and that those coming in had been stopped. (We now remembered having seen a regiment of French soldiers setting out from Poperinghe at the same time as we had done, and then they were suddenly stopped, while we went on and saw them no more.)

Despite what the sentinel told us, we remained unpersuaded. Seeing several soldiers going in and out of a house just opposite, we thought it would be as well to ask a temporary shelter till the bombardment should lessen. We ventured to ask admission, when what was our surprise to receive the warmest of welcomes and the kindest offers of hospitality. We could not have found a better spot. The family was thoroughly Christian; and, in this time of distress, the door of the house stood open day and night for all who were in need. How much more for nuns, and more especially enclosed nuns like ourselves! They had seen us passing on our way to Poperinghe, just a fortnight before, and had accompanied our wanderings with a prayer. A few days ago they had also given refreshment to the Poor Clares who had taken refuge at Vlamertinghe; and now their only desire was that God would spare their little house, that they might continue their deeds of mercy and true charity.

To give us pleasure, they introduced an Irish gentleman who was stopping with them, since the Germans had chased him out of Courtrai. A lively conversation soon began, while the good woman of the house prepared us a cup of hot coffee and some bread and butter. After this, the Irish gentleman, whose name was Mr. Walker, went out to investigate, to see if it would not be possible for us to continue our walk.

After about half an hour's absence, during which we were entertained by our host (M. Vanderghote, 10 Chaussée de Poperinghe, Ypres), who made his five children and two nieces come in to say goodnight to us before going to bed, Mr. Walker returned, saying it was a sheer impossibility to enter the town that evening, as the shells were falling at the rate of two every three minutes. He had called on M. l'Abbé Neuville, the priest above mentioned, Director of the Asylum, who said he would give us beds for the night, and then we could assist at his Mass at 6.30 next morning. The latter part of the proposition we gladly accepted; but as to the first, we were afraid of abusing his goodness, and preferred, if our first benefactor would consent, to remain where we were until morning.

Our host was only too pleased, being sorry that he could not provide us with beds. He then forced us to accept a good plate of warm butter-milk; after which, provided with blankets and shawls, we made ourselves as comfortable as we could for the night. Needless to say, we did not sleep very well and were entertained, till early morning, with explosions of bombs and shells, and the replying fire of the Allies' guns.

Once a vigorous rattling of the door-handle aroused us, but we were soon reassured by hearing M. Vanderghote inviting the poor half-frozen soldier, who had thus disturbed us, to go to the kitchen to take something warm. Before 6, we began to move, and performed our ablutions as best we could. The eldest son of the family now came to fetch us, to show us the way to the church of the asylum, where we had the happiness of hearing Holy Mass and receiving Holy Communion. When Mass was over we wound our way once more through the dimly-lit cloisters of the asylum, while we could not help smiling at the apparent appropriateness of the place we had chosen with the foolhardy act we were undertaking—of risking our lives in thus entering a town which even our brave troops had been obliged to evacuate.

Once outside the asylum, we found Mr. Walker waiting for us, with the eldest daughter and three sons of M. Vanderghote, who were pushing a hand-cart. We set off at a brisk pace along the frozen road. Passing by a few French soldiers, who looked amazed at our apparition, we soon entered the doomed town.

There, a truly heart-breaking sight awaited us. Broken-down houses, whose tottering walls showed remains of what had once been spacious rooms—buildings, half-demolished, half-erect,—met our wondering gaze everywhere. Windows, shattered in a thousand pieces, covered the ground where we walked; while, in the empty casements, imagination pictured the faces of hundreds of starving, homeless poor, whose emaciated features seemed to cry to heaven for vengeance on the heartless invaders of their peaceful native land.

But we durst not stop; the thought ever uppermost in our hearts was our own beloved abbey. How should we find it? We pushed on as quickly as we could, but the loose stones, bricks, beams and glass made walking a difficult matter, and twice, having passed halfway down a street, we were obliged to retrace our steps, owing to the road being entirely blocked by overthrown buildings. Here and there, we saw some poor creature looking half-frightened, half-amazed at seeing us, while suddenly turning a corner we came to a pool of frozen water, where three street boys were amusing themselves sliding on the ice. Their mirth seemed almost blameful among so many trophies of human misery! We now came in sight of St. Peter's Church, which at first glance appeared untouched; but coming round, past the Calvary, we saw that the porch had been struck.

One moment more, and we were in La Rue St. Jacques—nay, in front of our dear old home. The pavements were covered with debris of all kinds, but the other buildings had largely contributed to the pile. We hardly dared to raise our eyes; yet the monastery was there as before, seemingly untouched, save for the garrets over the nuns' cells, where the shell had burst before we had left. We were now greeted by a familiar voice, and looking round found the poor girl, Hélène, who was anxiously enquiring if we were returning to the convent. But there was no time to waste. The Germans, who had stopped bombarding Ypres at about 3 a.m., might recommence at any moment, and then we should have to fly; so we went to the door of the director's house to try to get into the abbey.

What was our astonishment to find Oscar, our old servant-man, there. Probably he was still more astonished than we, for he had never dared to come to the convent since he had left, and would surely feel, at the least, uncomfortable at our unexpected arrival. However, it was certainly not the moment to think of all these things, so we went in. The whole building seemed but one ruin. In the drawing-room, where the priest's breakfast things—laid a fortnight before—were still on the table, the ceiling was literally on the floor; the staircase was quite blocked with cement, mortar, wall-paper, and bricks; the sacristy, where we were assembled when the first shell fell, was untouched. The church, except for some five or six holes in the roof, was as we left it; but the altar, stripped of all that had once made it so dear to us, spoke volumes to our aching hearts.

Mounting the seven steps which led into the choir, we found ourselves once more in that beloved spot. The windows on the street side were in atoms; otherwise, all was intact. Our dearest Lord had watched over His House, His Royal State Chamber, where He was always ready to hold audience with His Beloved Spouses. We tore ourselves away, and flew to secure our breviaries, great-habits, and other things which the other nuns had recommended to us. Everywhere we went, dust and dirt covered the rooms, while a great many windows were broken. The statues of Our Blessed Lady and St. Joseph were unharmed, as also those of Our Holy Father St. Benedict and our Holy Mother St. Scholastica. Little Jesus of Prague had His crown at His feet, instead of on His head; one crucifix was broken in two! The cells were almost quite destroyed, big holes in the ceilings, the windows broken, the plaster down, frozen pools of water on the floor. We hastened to the garrets, where things were still worse.

The roof in this part was completely carried away, leaving full entrance to hail, snow, and rain; strong rafters and beams, which seemed made to last unshaken till the end of the world, were rent asunder or thrown on the floor; the huge iron weights of the big clock had rolled to the other end of the garrets; the scene of destruction seemed complete. We turned away; the other part looked secure, the apples and pears lying rotting away on the floors, where we had put them to ripen. In the noviceship, the ceiling was greatly damaged; whilst down in the cloisters, by the grotto of our Lady of Lourdes, a bomb had perforated the roof, the grotto remaining untouched. These seemed to be the principal effects of the invaders' cruelty, as far as our abbey was concerned.

We now came across our old carpenter, who had also come into the house with Oscar, and who had already put up planks on the broken windows in the choir, promising to do all he could to preserve the building. He also told us that one of the biggest German bombs had fallen in the garden, but had not exploded, so the French police had been able to take it away— another mark of God's loving care over us; for, had the bomb burst, it would have utterly destroyed our monastery. We were now obliged to leave. When should we see the dear old spot again? and in what state would it be if we ever did return?

The Return Journey to Poperinghe

The hand-cart being overloaded, we had to carry some of the things ourselves; and we must have looked a strange sight, carrying books and clothes, stuffed in white pillowcases—even Mr. Walker had one, which he hoisted on his shoulder. We did not trouble about this, but silently made our way back, through the deserted streets. We left the town by a different way from that by which we had entered it, as a sinister boom from the station warned us of the presence of the enemy. Our road took us this time through the Grand' Place. The whole back part of the hospital was destroyed; and although the walls of the *façade* were still standing, one could see, through the empty windows, that the interior was almost entirely demolished.

The Cloth Hall, also, had not been spared, one corner being severely damaged, and the greater number of the statues maimed and mutilated. If it could have remained so, there might have been some consolation; but now everyone knows the ruthless barbarity which has prompted the Huns of the twentieth century to utterly destroy this wonderful monument of medieval architecture, of which Ypres had been so justly proud during hundreds of years. It appears that the belfry, the chimes of which were only surpassed by those of Bruges and Antwerp, was struck just twenty-four hours after we had passed it on our exit from the town.

St. Martin's, too, had also been struck. We would, nevertheless, have entered, but Mr. Walker was afraid to let us prolong our stay, as the shells were already flying over us. Our thoughts naturally turned to the much revered and esteemed M. le Doyen, who, victim of his heroic courage, had remained at his post to the last, tending the wounded, and even helping to extinguish the fires which the incendiary bombs caused in so many places; till at last, seeing the interior of his beloved church already in flames, he had fallen, struck down by a cerebral congestion, and had been carried to the Dean of Poperinghe in the ambulance car. (Since, we have heard that he is better, D. G., one of our old pupils having seen him in the church at Poperinghe.)

On emerging from the town, a little incident occurred.

We came up with a British cavalry regiment. They were coming from the trenches. They looked at us and shouted: "Who are you, Sisters, and where do you come from?" Dame Columban answered: "We are English nuns from the Benedictine Convent of the Rue St. Jacques," This was too much for Dame Patrick, who called out: "We are no such thing. We are *Irish* Benedictines!"

"Irish!" shouted half a dozen of them, "and so are we," and they all began singing, "It's a long way to Tipperary," and, thus escorted, we took a long, last look at the dear old town. Needless to say, it was an Irish regiment—every man wore the harp and shamrock on his collar and cap.

We soon arrived at the house where we had taken refuge during the night, and were not sorry to have a good cup of coffee and some bread and butter and jam. Mr. Walker had told us of some of his experiences, among which was the burning of Madame la Baronne Coppens' house, this lady being the mother of one of our former pupils. M. Vanderghote's eldest son had been left in charge of their house, sleeping in the cellar at night.

On one occasion when the bombardment was raging fiercely, Mr. Walker had offered to accompany him. They kept watch in turns. As Mr. Walker was sleeping, the son woke him suddenly crying out, "Quick! get up! the house is on fire!" Half-dazed, he had seized hold of his candlestick and followed the son to the door. All was in flames. They turned back, half-stifled with the smoke, but could find no exit. At last they managed to break the glass of the window, and jumping out, just escaped from the place as, with a loud crash, the roof fell in. Mr. Walker had his candlestick still in his hand, which he showed us among pieces of shrapnel and shells, all souvenirs of the war. They had also saved the dog, which was slightly burnt.

We now hurried the preparations for our departure, as time

was passing quickly, and we had still a long walk before us. Our kind host accompanied us as far as the cross-roads where the French police mounted guard, for he was not allowed farther. By a strange coincidence we met once more the Belgian officer who had seen us the evening before. He was more than astonished at what we had done, and was very pleased that all had succeeded so well. We thanked Monsieur Vanderghote warmly for all that he had done for us, promising that, if it were possible, we should assuredly call on him on our return to Ypres. We then set off, two of us pushing the cart.

We had taken but a few steps, when a French official stopped us once more, saying that no carts were allowed on the highroad, except those belonging to the army. We had therefore to take a country lane, which had the double inconvenience of being twice as long as the straight road and, indeed, of being also almost impassable. However, there was nothing to be done but to go forward as best we could; so off we went. Oh dear! One wanted Goliath's strength to push the cart over the stones and ruts. After a few yards we came to a dead stop. The cart was stuck. We pushed and pushed with might and main—vain efforts. We could not move it. We were finally obliged to pull backwards, and thus managed to extricate it.

Taught by experience, we took more care next time, looking where we were going to; so things went pretty well for about a hundred paces, when, glancing behind us, what was our dismay to see a number of French soldiers coming by the same road, some on horseback, others on foot, others driving carts. There was only the narrow lane in front of us, with no means of turning visible to the right or left. What was to be done? We hurried on as best we could, but what was the use?—in ten minutes they would surely overtake us.

At last, turning round a corner, what was our relief to see an open gateway leading into a farmyard. We boldly pushed our precious load in, thus leaving room for the soldiers to pass. We then tried if it were possible to find someone to help us; because, judging from the difficulties we had met with so far, it was really questionable if we should arrive at Poperinghe before evening. After grumbling a bit, two men offered to come with us as far as Vlamertinghe. This was better than nothing; and, as we followed them, we fervently prayed that we should meet with someone else later on.

On we trudged, wondering what had happened in the convent since our departure. What if the Belgian *commandant* had found a train, and everyone had been obliged to leave without us! No, surely that was not possible. We passed soldiers, men, women, children, wading through pools of mud and water, and lamenting our long detour, which had made us waste so much precious time. Vlamertinghe at last—still five long miles to Poperinghe—should we *ever* get there? On arriving at the village, our two good fellows set about finding someone else to push our cart, and finally succeeded. Having paid them, we set off once more on our journey, when behold! a barrier was placed across the road, and we had to come to a standstill. They told us a train was coming. We looked and looked, but saw no sign of it in either direction.

Meanwhile a crowd of people assembled, who, accustomed to such proceedings, pushed past, right up to the railing, to be the first to pass, and we were left at the back. We waited and waited, still no train. What a waste of time! Then came the sound of horses' hoofs, and up trotted a whole regiment of soldiers, who, of course, rode to the front, pushing the crowd back, and us along with them. Still no train! We now happened to look across to the other side of the barrier, and discovered another regiment, waiting on the opposite side, with again a crowd of people behind them. Should we ever get through? Still no train!

Decidedly, the good man's watch must have been considerably in advance, or else he possessed the virtue of prudence in its highest perfection. At length a feeble whistle told us that the long-expected locomotive was coming. But it must have been a train of wounded soldiers; for first it moved forward at a snail's pace, and secondly it seemed, to our worn-out patience, to be at least one mile in length. However, it passed at last; and, the barriers being withdrawn, the two regiments crossed four abreast, then the crowds pushed through, and last but not least came the representatives of the Irish Benedictine Abbey, with their stylish-looking hand-cart. Once more, on we pushed; but the five miles must have been German ones, which, like their dreadful soldiers, never come to an end.

Our guide kept bravely on, from time to time stopping to wipe the perspiration off his face; for, although it was freezing, the poor fellow had no light work to try to advance through the mud and dirt. At last, passing by some houses, he left the cart in the middle of the road, and vanished. The reason soon became evident, for a moment afterwards he came out with a glass of foaming beer, wherewith to refresh himself. Once again, on we went. Would the road ever come to an end? Would we ever arrive at our destination? We scanned the horizon to find some vestige of our approaching goal, but could discover nothing but an endless succession of trees, hop-gardens, fields.

Finally, however, some houses came in sight, so plucking up our courage, we pushed forward, and soon reached the convent door. At last we should get a rest. Alas, how we were deceiving ourselves! Once inside, we were soon surrounded by our sisters, one more anxious than the other to know what had happened, and to tell us what had been decided during our absence. Parcels of every shape and dimension next met our eyes. Arrived at the room which we generally occupied, what was our astonishment to find dear Lady Abbess downstairs, surrounded by the nuns of both communities. On catching sight of us, she was more than delighted. We knelt for her blessing, and to tell her some of our adventures, and then learnt the reason of all this excitement.

Mother Prioress will now tell what happened during the absence of Dame Columban, Dame Patrick, and Dame Placid.

As soon as the three nuns had set out for Ypres, we went to the chapel to recommend them to the protection of God, and by a fervent "*Sub tuum*" we commended them to the care of the Blessed Virgin. They had promised me to be back if possible that night, or at least the next morning, if they could remain in the convent cellars without too much danger. At 3 p.m. I was called to see Captain Liddell, who told me that the British Headquarters would place two ambulance cars at our disposal to conduct Lady Abbess and the community to St. Omer. The cars would be ready between ten and eleven next morning. He also said that, once at St. Omer, I had only to address myself to the mayor, or to the general staff. I thanked him profusely, and told him of my anxiety for the three nuns who had gone to Ypres. "It was a very imprudent thing to attempt," he answered.

"I trust they will not be allowed to enter the town, for it is being fiercely shelled."

I was very alarmed, as were the rest of the community, to whom I related what the captain had said. In the evening, we were assembled with the nuns from Oostmieunkerke in the big parlour, which the Superioress had kindly allotted for our use. The gas being cut off, we had only one *pétrole* lamp between us. We spent our time working and praying.

From time to time, on hearing a ring at the bell, we would ask if the nuns had yet come back; one of the younger nuns would go and enquire, but always returned disappointed. We looked at each other anxiously. What would become of them this night? We could only recommend them to God. Suddenly I had an inspiration. "Let us put them under the protection of St. Raphael," I said, "and promise him a Mass tomorrow—there are several priests at the ambulance, one of them will surely be free to say it." Everyone was pleased with the idea, and Dame Teresa went to make enquiries. She soon came back in triumph, saying that the priest from Avignon was outside. We told him our distress, and respectfully begged him to be so kind as to say the Mass in honour of St. Raphael for the safe return of our three absent ones. He willingly agreed. At the same moment the appearance of the *portress* brought the cry to our lips: "They are there!"

"No! it is the Commandant Delporte, of the Belgian police, who wishes to speak to Mother Prioress." I went to the parlour, fear and hope alternately taking possession of my heart. He came to ask if Captain Liddell had called, and if the decision of the headquarters suited us. I told him of the arrangement and added, "Once at St. Omer, what shall I do with our honoured Lady Abbess? May she remain in the motor, which they say must return to Poperinghe that evening, while I go to the mayor and general staff."

He reflected a moment, and then, taking one of his cards, he wrote a few words recommending us to Major Kirke. " Take this," he said, rising, "and give it to the major, who is a great friend of mine, and rest assured that all will be well." I could not thank him enough, and conducted him to the door. There I found myself in presence of two men, who asked to see me. They brought me a message from our nuns, telling me not to be anxious; they would not return that night, but the next day, as soon as possible. I felt a little relieved, but again the question presented itself, at what hour would they arrive? Would they be in time? The next morning we arranged our modest parcels, which—thanks to the dexterity of Dame Aloysius—were soon ready, thinking all the time of our missing sisters. For my part, I went to prepare Lady Abbess for our departure, for the hour was fast approaching. We must come to a decision—the three must remain at La Sainte Union until the opportunity of joining us in England should present itself.

We had now to get Lady Abbess down the stairs which were narrow and steep, and it was with the greatest difficulty that we succeeded. We made her as comfortable as we could in an armchair in the big parlour, where the nuns of the three communities gathered round her, for everyone was filled with an affectionate respect for her, mingled with compassion for her age and infirmity. We tried to hide our perplexity and anxiety from her. It was now time to start, and the three were not yet back. At this moment the *portress* entered the room smiling—what was it? Captain Liddell had just called to say the motors would not be round till 1.30. "*Deo gratias!*" To complete our happiness, the absent ones soon arrived, covered with dust and mud, but producing in triumph the great-habits and breviaries they had been able to save.

CHAPTER 12

On The Way to England

There was now no time to waste. The few treasures we had brought with us were promptly added to the other packages; while it was decided that each nun should wear her great-habit, as much to lessen the number of parcels, as to preserve us from the cold, especially when crossing the sea. We bade *adieu* to the Superioress and community of La Sainte Union, who had given us such a warm welcome, and shown us such hospitality during the past fortnight. They asked us in return to beseech Our Lord not to allow the Germans to bombard Poperinghe, that they might be able to stop in their convent, which they had only built during the past eleven years, since the French Government had driven them from Hazebrouck.

A ring at the door interrupted our *adieux*. The voice of a British officer was heard, asking if this were the convent where the Irish Dames of Ypres had taken refuge. The answer was soon given; and while some went to help Lady Abbess, others seized the 'baggage,' and all were soon at the door, where a group of wondering children and other people were assembled to see what would be the end of such an unusual sight. The great difficulty was to get our venerable invalid into the car; for although able to walk fairly well when helped on both sides, it was almost impossible for her to mount the two small steps. However, the soldiers soon came to the rescue; and, with the help of their strong arms, she was soon established comfortably in a corner of one of the motors, enveloped in a blanket and numerous shawls to keep out the cold. The rest of the community were not long in getting in the motors, and Edmund brought up the rear with a young Irish girl, Miss Keegan, who had been trying to get home since the war broke out, and had now begged to be allowed to make the journey with us.

Owing to the heavy fall of rain and the unusual traffic, the roads were in a very bad condition and consequently our ride was not of the smoothest; but no accident occurred. Being frosty weather, the wind was bitterly cold, and we were obliged to keep everything closed that Lady Abbess might not be inconvenienced. She, however, kept up bravely. We did not forget to say the '*Sub tuum*,' nor to invoke our good St. Raphael with a fervent '*Angeli, archangeli*,' to which we added the prayer for travellers. About halfway our kind guides came round to the entrance of the cars to know if we wanted anything.

We passed through several villages and small towns surrounded by snow-covered fields and frozen ponds. Nothing of note happened to vary the monotony of the continual shaking of our motors. A little after 5 p.m. we came to a standstill, and looking out, found ourselves in what seemed to be a good-sized town. We were not left long in suspense, for soon the cheery face of the officer in charge appeared, enquiring where we wished to be driven, for we were at St. Omer. Mother Prioress then produced the letter of recommendation given her by Commandant Delporte for Major Kirke. The officer took the card, and soon we moved off in another direction.

After a few minutes' run, we came again to a halt, stopping some time. The officer then reappeared, saying that the major was absent, and asking where we would like to go now. Alas! we did not know, and wondered if it would not be advisable to go straight on to Boulogne that same evening, to take the boat the first thing next morning. The officer, seeing our perplexity, vanished once more. Soon we were bowling through busy streets, lined with shops well lit. Another stop, a few minutes' wait, and off we were again. A third halt—then another officer appeared, saluted, and asked in excellent French if he could render us any service, or replace Major Kirke, who was absent from St. Omer. On hearing our situation, he told us that if we would just step out we should find accommodation in the establishment before which the cars had stopped. As he was still speaking, the persons who kept the house came out, helping us down, taking the parcels from us, and seeming more than delighted at our arrival.

We were not sorry to leave the cars, for we were quite cramped with the long, cold drive. The next question was how to get Lady Abbess out of her corner, and into the house. At last the officer in charge had the bright idea of carrying her on a stretcher. Accordingly, one was brought down and laid on the seat opposite. We then helped her to sit on the stretcher, and induced her to lie down. She was at first afraid, not being accustomed to this novel mode of conveyance; but, being reassured, she allowed the soldiers to carry her into the house, and she was soon seated in a comfortable arm-chair by a blazing fire. After expressing our gratitude to the good soldiers, we rejoined Lady Abbess and soon made acquaintance with our kind hostesses. What was our delight to find that they were secularised Ursuline nuns, and that the house had formerly been a convent of La Sainte Union. It is therefore unnecessary to state that we were received with the greatest charity, a bed being even carried down to the room where we were for Lady Abbess, so that she should not be obliged to go upstairs. Poor Edmund had once more to be sent off, being conducted to almost the other end of the town, much to his distress.

After a good supper, we retired to rest in what had once been the children's dormitory, and fatigued by such an eventful day we slept well. Next morning we were awakened by the deep tones of church bells. They were ringing the 6 o'clock Mass in the cathedral, which was quite close to the convent. We arose, and arrived in time for a late Mass. We were shown to seats almost at the top of the church. After a few moments we heard the sound of soldiers marching, and soon we had to give place to them, for we had come to a Military Mass, celebrated by an army chaplain. Two by two the soldiers advanced, being marshalled to right and left by an officer. It was an Irish regiment, and there were altogether about seventy soldiers who attended devoutly to Holy Mass, and more than one, when the moment of Holy Communion came, mingled with those who approached the altar.

After Mass, we were conducted back to the convent, promising ourselves a visit during the day to see the many objects of devotion and interest in the venerable cathedral. We were not disappointed. Amongst other antiquities is a 'Descent from the Cross' by Rubens, and oil-paintings in memory of a visit which holy King Louis IX and Charles X paid to the cathedral, in thanksgiving for the success of their arms. The sacred vessels, also, were for the most part of great antiquity, especially a very ancient *pyx* ornamented with filigree work. Besides the high altar, in the middle of the sanctuary, having the stalls for the bishop and canons behind, there were numerous side-altars, among which the most remarkable was that dedicated to Our Blessed Lady of Miracles.

This miraculous statue was held in great veneration by the inhabitants of the town; and in the great peril they had gone through some weeks past, when the Germans were advancing on St. Omer, and when the British had saved it by arriving only just in time—for had they come but half an hour later, the enemy would have been before them—in the moment of peril, the people had promised Our Blessed Lady, to give a new bell to the cathedral if she kept the dreaded invaders from entering the city. '*Ex-votos*' without end hung all round the altar, besides numberless engravings in thanksgiving for miracles and cures obtained through Our Lady's intercession.

After our interesting visit, we stopped for vespers, which, since the beginning of the War, were sung by the entire congregation; during which time we profited to say our own *vespers* and *compline*. We then went to visit M. le Curé de Furnes who, we knew, was stopping at St. Omer, Mother Prioress desiring to have news of her cousin the Dean of Furnes who, we heard, was at Boulogne. We also had the pleasure of saluting M. le Vicaire.

On our way, we met some soldiers from Morocco—easily distinguished as Arabs, by their bright blue tunics and long scarlet cloaks, with their big turbans, their blankets thrown round them, and their lovely horses. When we returned to the house, we learned that Lieutenant Stuart-Hayes, who had been so kind to us on the previous evening, had called to see Reverend Mother. He had, likewise, left a message to say that he would try to assist at Benediction in the evening; and afterwards he would come round again. He would be also very grateful if, before his visit, Mother Prioress would make out all that was necessary for our passports.

All being finished, we set out for the cathedral once again; for although there were still twenty minutes before Benediction, yet at St. Omer, as nearly everywhere else, the churches, since the beginning of hostilities, were crowded, and those who before never put their foot inside a church were now amongst the most fervent; so, to secure our places, we had to be there in time. The rosary was first said aloud, the priest ascending the pulpit, so as to be better heard by everyone.

After the 'O *Salutaris*,' repeated alternately by the choir and congregation, the '*Miserere*' was sung, the people repeating the first lines between each verse of the Psalm. There was something particularly touching in that cry for mercy which arose from every heart at the thought of the dear ones who, perhaps even at that very moment, were being shot down on the battlefield. But what made the most impression was the hymn sung after Benediction, and which still rings in our ears—that ardent supplication to '*La bonne Mère!*' '*Vierge d'espéranee, Étends sur nous ton voile; Sauve, sauve la France! Ne l'abandonne pas!*' It was truly a prayer in the real sense of the word, beseeching the Mother of Mercy not to forsake the land she had so many times miraculously saved, and where, but a short while before, had been seen such a wonderful outburst of faith at the Eucharistic Congress of Lourdes—the spot chosen by Our Blessed Lady herself, and where the devotion to the Son had ever been united to that of the Mother. The sound of the grand old organ greatly enhanced the beauty of the singing; and our hearts also mounted to the throne of mercy in behalf of our well-beloved Abbey which we were now leaving so far behind.

Soon afterwards, returning to our lodgings. Mother Prioress received the promised visit of the lieutenant, accompanied by a military priest. He brought all the necessary papers with him, together with a recommendation for the Governor of Boulogne, and took away our passports to have them signed. Reverend Mother told him she would like so much to have a Mass celebrated the next day in honour of St. Raphael for our safe voyage. He promised to see if it would be possible; and true enough, he returned a short time after with the good news that not only should we have a Mass said at which we could assist, but that he had obtained permission for the priest to accompany us as far as Boulogne. We were now in jubilation and proceeded once more to arrange our packages.

The night soon passed, and next morning we proceeded to the cathedral wondering where we should find 'our priest,' whom we did not know, and had never seen! At the High Altar preparations were being made for a funeral; so we passed to the chapel of Our Lady of Miracles where a Mass was already half finished, hoping that 'our priest' would perhaps say the next one. Towards the end, he came himself to look for us, and told us he would not be able to come to Our Lady's Altar as all the Masses there were reserved, but that he would commence immediately at St. Antony's. So we crossed over to the other side of the cathedral where Father Flynn (as we afterwards found out he was called) said Mass, at which we all received Holy Communion.

After breakfast we made the last preparations; and, about ten, three ambulance cars drove up to the house. The exiled nuns helped us as much as they could, giving us each a postcard with a view of the convent as a souvenir of our visit. They were sorry to see us leave, and told us to be sure and call on them again, if we should ever repass by St. Omer. The soldiers now came in with a stretcher for Lady Abbess; and the nuns were so good that they insisted on lending a mattress, blankets, and pillows, which would be returned with the cars. Having placed Lady Abbess on this portable bed, the soldiers carried her out with the greatest care. Father Flynn presiding and enlivening the whole proceeding with Irish wit. We were soon seated in the cars, but had some time to wait, as Mother Prioress was obliged to get a little money changed.

Meanwhile several people came to speak to us, among whom was the sister of one of our former pupils, who, recognising our habit, came forward to know what had happened to the abbey. After a little while Reverend Mother returned; but still the cars did not start. We soon learnt the reason when Lieutenant Stuart-Hayes appeared triumphantly with a bottle of light wine and a box of biscuits, which he insisted on our accepting. We could not thank him enough for all that he had done for us; but he withdrew immediately, after making sure we had all we desired, and courteously saluting us, he gave word for the motors to start and we were soon on the road to Boulogne.

It was bitterly cold, so we kept the car in which Lady Abbess was lying well covered. Just outside St. Omer, a British aeroplane mounted from the aviation field. This was the last we saw of active hostilities. Father Flynn kept the conversation going, and, between the prayers and hymns, endeavoured to enliven the company. He told us he was the first Catholic chaplain to arrive with the troops in France. He was going to the front on the following Wednesday—let us hope that he will be spared.

After running along for some time as smoothly as was possible, considering the bad state of the roads, the inmates of one of the motors heard a crack like a report of a revolver. At the same instant the car stood stock-still—the two others following necessarily did likewise. On enquiry, it was discovered that a tyre had burst, which meant a little halt on the way. As we were just outside a village, the inhabitants, though accustomed by this time to British soldiers passing by, were not accustomed to seeing nuns with them and consequently crowded round to examine us a little nearer. None being brave enough to ask where we came from, they solved the problem themselves, and christened us 'Les Petites Soeurs de la Croix Rouge,' a title which I am afraid we hardly deserved.

The country through which we passed seemed very picturesque, judging from the glimpses we got from time to time by lifting up the flap at the end of the car—fields covered with snow gradually sinking in gentle slopes or rising in the distance in hilly ranges. From time to time a woody glade would change the monotony of the succeeding meadows, then a small village with its quaint little houses. As we were thus putting more and more distance between Belgium and ourselves, a sudden crash soon broke the reigning silence. The leading motor having drawn up when at full speed, the two others—not expecting this—had run one on top of the other. We were all thrown over on our seats and so remained, not daring to move, for fear of what might happen next.

The truth was that the first car, owing to a rapid run down a slippery hill had charged into a telegraph post, and that was the cause of our being roused so unceremoniously out of the dreams of 'auld lang syne.' The drivers soon appeared to make excuses for the fright they had unwillingly given us, saying that there was no harm done, except for a window broken. We were quite reassured and started off again. Lady Abbess had fortunately not realised the danger, and only asked what the noise meant, and why we had stopped.

We rolled on once more, but our guides soon came to the conclusion that they had mistaken their way; so, consulting their maps, they turned back. Uphill and down again, going at the same flying pace, we at last arrived in the historic old town of Boulogne. There we still continued to mount and descend, for the streets seemed all very steep. It was now between 2.30 and 3 p.m. and the boat would not leave till 4. We decided it would be better to stop in our cars, as it was hardly according to the nature of our vocation to go about sight-seeing, and if we got down we should only stand shivering in the cold.

The motorcar in which were Lady Abbess and Mother Prioress was next driven off to the governor's house, and having drawn up. Father Flynn alighted to arrange everything for us. We patiently awaited his return, little dreaming of the honour which was being prepared for us, till we saw the governor coming in person to salute the Superioress. Reverend Mother having returned his greeting, told him of the great kindness we had everywhere received from the British Headquarters, at which he expressed the hope that we would experience the same from the French. He then introduced Lieutenant Treillard, to whom he gave us in charge, with directions to see us all safely on board. With truly French gallantry the lieutenant saluted the company, and Father Flynn carefully pocketing his precious papers and jumping up by the chauffeur, the car with Lady Abbess and Mother Prioress rejoined the rest of the community.

Our conductors, who were evidently hungry, now produced bread, tinned meat, and cheese. One, buying some potato chips, promptly came to share them with us. We declined to accept them, thanking him all the same for his kindness. We thought we could not do better than follow their example; so Mother Prioress divided Lieutenant Stuart-Hayes' biscuits among us. Father Flynn produced a packet of chocolate, and then each in turn drank some wine from the solitary little mug we had brought in case Lady Abbess should want anything on the way. As the soldiers seemed very cold, stamping their feet on the frozen road, Reverend Mother gave them also a drop of wine; and for one who refused (having probably taken the pledge) she warmed some milk with the little spirit-lamp we had. They were all delighted. Poor fellows! it was the least we could do for them, when they had rendered us such good service.

Captain Dwyer, who had brought our papers from the general staff to Lieutenant Stuart-Hayes when we were at St. Omer, now joined us once more (having been sent to Boulogne with despatches) to assure himself of our safety. Our long stay ended by exciting the curiosity of the bystanders, and we received rather indiscreet visits of persons who, apparently passing innocently by the cars, lifted up the flap to look in. Some ventured to talk, and we discovered one poor man who said he came from the Rue St. Jacques, Ypres, and an old woman who had walked all the way from Dixmude.

At last it was time to go on board the boat. The ambulance cars took us quite close to the gangway. When we had all got down with our parcels, the soldiers lifted the stretcher on which Lady Abbess was lying, and gently carried her on board and into the cabin, where we helped her on to a sofa. Lieutenant Treillard superintended everything, and good Father Flynn made fun all the time. The latter then gave special injunctions to Reverend Mother about the papers, &c., and giving us his blessing, with a special one to Lady Abbess, having in his turn begged hers, with all possible wishes for a safe arrival at our destination, he hurried off the boat, which was preparing to leave. The passage was very calm, but cold and frosty. For more than one of us it was the first crossing, Lady Abbess having up to this time never even seen the sea; and, sad to say, nearly all proved 'bad sailors' except, curiously enough, Lady Abbess. Happily, however, the passage only lasted 1 hr. 20 min., so we were soon at Folkestone.

Thanks to our papers from British and French Headquarters, we were passed successfully by the doctor and other officials (who stopped two Belgian peasants following us ashore)—even Edmund got through without the least difficulty. Arrived in the station, a telegram was sent to a relative of one of the community in London, who kindly looked out lodgings for us in advance. It seemed an interminable time before the train set off, and afterwards, rushing through the darkness, passing station after station, town after town, we thought London would never come. However, all things come to an end, and so did our journey, as at last we steamed into Victoria Station.

There, one would have said we were expected, we were so kindly received by the ladies on the platform, who helped us out and pressed us to take something. On hearing where we had come from, and how we had succeeded in getting honoured Lady Abbess safe through so many difficulties, everyone was more than interested; and soon porters were running in all directions to get cabs to convey us to our destination which was in quite another part of London. A bath-chair was brought for Lady Abbess who was wheeled out of the station, Mother Prioress holding her hand.

One of the ladies, seeing the impossibility of getting her into a cab, fetched a private motorcar. The gentleman who owned it, helped by a soldier, lifted Lady Abbess gently in. Then they drove to the hospital of SS. John and Elizabeth, whither it was thought better for the present to take Lady Abbess. The soldier, overcome by the sight of our dear abbess' patience, took her in his arms—exclaiming, when he came downstairs, 'I could not help it, she is such a dear good old lady.' Dame Patrick's aunt (Mrs. Adamson) had arranged everything for us, and so Dame Patrick, with Mother Prioress and Dame Columban, were cordially received at her house.

Lady Abbess remained at the hospital of SS. John and Elizabeth, where, indeed, she received every attention, together with seven other members of the community. Dame Teresa, Dame Aloysius, and Dame Walburge experienced the same charity at the Sisters of Hope. Edmund was also taken in at Mrs. Adamson's. Those at the hospital and the Sisters of Hope heard Mass there next morning; and Mother Prioress, Dame Columban, and Dame Patrick walked as far as the Dominicans at Haverstock Hill. We may here note the loving goodness of Divine Providence, which had not once allowed us to miss Mass or Holy Communion in spite of all the dangers and fatigues of the past weeks. We were truly like the Israelites in the desert, for whom the *manna* never failed.

CHAPTER 13

Oulton

Next morning we were all motored from our different lodgings to Euston Station, where we were met by Mr. Nolan, brother of Rev. Dom Nolan, O.S.B., and at 10.30 we entered on the last stage of our never-to-be-forgotten journey. We had three reserved compartments at our disposal, by the kind intervention of a gentleman at Victoria Station, who had given a signed card to Mother Prioress, telling her to show it to anyone who should question her. And so we travelled safely from Ypres to Oulton. How strange it seemed, for more than one of us, to pass by those scenes which we had thought never more to see in this life! We had left our country, home, and all, to shut ourselves up in the peaceful solitude of Ypres Abbey; and here we were, forced to retrace our steps and to return temporarily to the world which we had willingly given up. God was, however, preparing us another place of refuge from the turmoil of Babylon, into which we had suddenly been thrown.

After changing trains at Stafford, where Lady Abbess experienced the same considerate compassion which had been shown to her all along, we arrived at Stone Station. There we were met by some of the pupils of Oulton Abbey, who told us how everyone was expecting us, and how they had tried during the past weeks to obtain news of us, but always unsuccessfully. Two Dominican nuns from the Stone Convent next came forward to greet us, one being an old Princethorpian school-companion of Dame Columban and Dame Teresa.

The carriages awaiting us were soon full, and as there was not room for all, four of us offered to walk. We lost nothing by this; for passing by Stone, the two Dominican nuns who had so kindly come to the station to meet us, obtained permission for us to visit their convent. We went all round the church (the community were singing

111

vespers in their choir) and then through the cloisters, which reminded us of the dear Abbey we had left behind. We saw the community room and several others, and lastly found ourselves in the parlour, where we awaited the honoured visit of Reverend Mother Prioress. We passed an agreeable time, till the sound of carriage wheels told us that one of the vehicles which had already been up to Oulton had returned to fetch us.

Our honoured Lady Abbess and the community were received with open arms at St. Mary's Abbey. It was with true motherly affection that Lady Laurentia opened the doors of her monastery to receive the Ypres community. The two communities—Oulton and Ypres—have always been closely united, and one of the first thoughts of the Oulton nuns, on the outbreak of this dreadful war in Belgium, was for the Abbey at Ypres. As early as September 17 the Lady Abbess had written and offered us a home, in case we had to leave our monastery; but for some weeks we had refused to believe that this would ever happen.

When we arrived we found the Lady Abbess and community assembled to receive us, and also the chaplain, Monsignor Schobel. who was no stranger, as he had often visited us at Ypres when staying with his friends at Bruges. We were very pleased to see him again.

By degrees we learned the trouble we had unwittingly caused the nuns; for a letter which Mother Prioress had written five days before, from Poperinghe, to announce our arrival had only come that morning, and the telegram from London had followed almost immediately. Everyone had been obliged to set to work to prepare for our accommodation. Two large rooms were placed at Lady Abbess' service. There were only two cells free, so one was allotted to Mother Prioress, and the other to Dame Placid. The rest of the choir dames were comfortably established in a dormitory of the new building only completed since the month of October. The lay-sisters found beds in another large room, and so our wanderings came to an end.

No one save those who have suffered as we have suffered can realise the joy which we experienced in finding ourselves once more in the calm and quiet of monastic life, where Holy Mass and Communion, the singing of the Divine Office, meditation and spiritual reading, succeeding the varied duties of the day, tend to soften the memories of the scenes of bloodshed and wretchedness which can never be forgotten.

Yet the echoes of this war of horrors reach us, even in our haven of rest. As I write, news reaches us from our chaplain (Monsieur de Seagher, *Principal du College Episcopal*, Ypres) who has returned to Ypres to find his college entirely pillaged and almost in ruins. He says that a third of the population has already re-entered the town; all are in dismay at the heartrending sight which meets their gaze. As to our convent, he writes:

> The state of your abbey is also deplorable. The shells have made great havoc there. The French soldiers occupy it at present. In several places the water is rising in the cellars. God alone knows what we shall still see, for the bombardment is not yet finished.

And now, what has God in store for us? We know not! When shall we return to brave little Belgium, and how shall we rebuild our monastery which, as has been said, should this very year celebrate its 250th anniversary? God, in His own good time, will raise up kind friends who will come to our assistance—of this we cannot doubt. In confidence, patience, and prayer we shall therefore await the moment chosen by Him Who has said: '*Seek first the Kingdom of God, and all these things (i.e.* temporal gifts) *shall be added to you.*'

Meanwhile we beg the Father of Mercy and the God of all Consolation to have pity on the world, and put an end to the dreadful punishment which weighs so heavily on our unfortunate generation. May He enlighten our enemies, that, realising the injustice of their cause, they may be converted, and cease their cruelties. May He also, in His infinite goodness, purge the entire universe from the crimes which have degraded humanity and brought it down to the level of ancient paganism, so that all, seeking only His greater honour and glory, may unite in the canticle of praise which Holy Church places on our lips during the Holy Sacrifice of the Mass, and which first resounded on Bethlehem's plains round the crib of our common Redeemer:—

'*Gloria in excelsis Deo, et in terra pax hominibus bonae voluntatis.*'

From Convent to Conflict

or

A Nun's Account of the Invasion of Belgium

Contents

Introduction

The publication of this little volume has for its object a better understanding of actual conditions, immediately following the invasion of a hostile army. The hope is indulged that the harrowing scenes witnessed by the author in Belgium, after the German invasion in 1914, may induce our own countrymen and women to more fully appreciate the blessings of peace. The events narrated are set forth as actually occurring, and—"*with malice to none, with charity for all.*"

Any profits derived from its favourable reception by the reading public or the charitably inclined are to be devoted to the reconstruction and repair of our school and convent, damaged during the engagement at the Fortress of Willebroeck, or for the establishment of a sewing school, with a lace-making department, for young women in America or England, as our Reverend Superiors may decide.

Any assistance in this charitable work will be gratefully appreciated by the author and her scattered community in Belgium, England and Holland.

Sister M. Antonia.

Skaneateles, New York,
April 3rd, 1916.

Letter of Introduction

La Supérieure du Couvent des Filles de Marie a Willebroeck, Province d'Anvers, en Belgique déclare par la présente que ses soeurs Marie An-toine et Marie Cecile sont envoyées aux Extats Unis, a fin d'examiner s'il y aurait noyen d'y établir une colonie de Filles de Marie; elle donne a Soeur M. Antoine le Pouvoir d'agir en son nom afin de prendre les mesures nécessaires a cet effet

Soeur M. Berchmans.

Willebroeck, 29 September, 1914.

Apprové:

D. J. Card. Mercier, Arch, de Malines

TRANSLATION.

The Superior of the Convent of the Daughters of Mary, Wil-lebroeck, Province of Antwerp, Belgium, state by this present (letter) that the Sisters Mary Antonia and Mary Cecilia are sent to the United States in order to examine if there are means of establishing a colony (mission) of the Daughters of Mary there; she gives to Sister M. Antonia the power to act in her name as to taking the measures necessary to this effect.

Sister M. Berchmans.

Willebroeck, 29 September, 19 14.

Approved:

D. J. Card. Mercier, Arch, de Malines.

CHAPTER 1

Boarding School in the Convent

At the Boarding School in the Couvent des Filles de Marie, Wille-broeck, Prov. d'Anvers, Belgique, July, 1914 a merry group of convent girls, in charge of sister guardian, was seated in the shade of a huge old pear tree, discussing the joys and expectations of the approaching summer vacation. High are the walls enclosing this ancient cloister, and many are the gay young hearts protected and developed within its shady precincts.

Bright are the faces and happy the hearts of more than one hundred young girls on this midsummer day in the memorable year 1914. They are now enjoying the morning air in the playground, having just returned from their usual walk in the garden. The weather is somewhat oppressive; but as time is precious in boarding school, everyone has something to do. One is crocheting; another is finishing a piece of Irish lace; still another is reviewing an article in a certain newspaper, as it is her task to make a summary for that evening's meeting of the Study Circle.

Joy, unalloyed by the experience of care or sorrow, is written on the face of every child. It is only one week before the annual distribution of prizes, the subsequent close of the school year, and a speedy family reunion.

It is eight o'clock. The sign is given, and instantly a hundred busybodies become still and serious. Not another word is spoken as the *preceptress* conducts the long line through the large playroom, over the small yard, and into the various classrooms.

The young ladies, aged from fifteen to twenty, proceed at once to the sewing department. This is to them the most important and interesting of all the rooms; needlework being a predominant feature in the education of all young Belgian women. After prayer, work begins.

Some are cutting patterns; others are putting pretty lace collars on those suits which must serve for the reception of diplomas; and a few of the more diligent, who have completed the term's work, are now finishing some lace or embroidery; while a cheery little canary is singing to the doubtful harmony of twenty sewing machines.

At the desk sits the patient and zealous teacher, Sister M. Alphonse, assisted in her work by two young novices. She is, perhaps, the most widely known and respected seamstress in all the province. For years her gold embroidery has sparkled on flags and banners; for years her skilful fingers have adorned the vestments that beautified God's altar in many churches of the diocese. Sister M. Alphonse knows the secret of winning the confidence of her pupils, and it is interesting to see how they crowd around her to reveal their little joys and sorrows and obtain advice in the various necessities of a long and busy school year.

On leaving the sewing-room, the visitor proceeds to the other departments. On all sides order and discipline prevail. The stone-floored halls are spotlessly clean. Pretty mosaic figures attract the eye and give a quaint appearance to those ancient corridors. The walls are very high, the rooms spacious, the windows long and broad, thus capable of admitting an abundance of air, light and sunshine. The wooden floors of the classrooms are often scrubbed and strewn with fine white sand from the seashore.

Sad is the lot of any poor child who might have the misfortune to upset an inkstand. You would find her on her knees rubbing the stain with soap and scraping it with a piece of glass until every vestige of ink disappears. If you tell her to be more careful in future, she will laughingly reply: *"Schuren is toch zoo aangenaam"* (scrubbing is so pleasant) .

In passing from one room to another, one notices the zeal and energy of both pupils and teachers. So busy are they, and so diligently are the hours employed, that the long school day, from eight o'clock in the morning until seven in the evening, fleets quickly away. The desks are stiff, and hard, and heavy; but no one complains. The young Belgian women are devoted to their country and its customs; and if one were told that in another country more comfortable desks were provided, she would answer candidly, *"Wij blijven liever in ons vaderland"* (We would rather remain in our *own* country).

The climate of Belgium is temperate, though more inclined to be cool than warm. The ground is very moist in some places. Never have we experienced the extremes of heat and cold found in America. Very heavy rains, accompanied by lightning and deafening peals of thunder, occur in the summer. There is little snow in the winter. In some parts of the country the grass is emerald green all year long. Rosebuds are seen on the bushes in January, and sometimes the trees are budding in February.

The stoves in Belgium are far inferior to those in America. Kitchen ranges are not used to bake bread. Those who do not possess stone or steam ovens, are obliged to buy bread daily at the baker's.

When accustomed to the cool, invigorating climate of Belgium, a great contrast is experienced in visiting America, and one feels more or less in danger of suffocation during a journey in an overheated rail-road car, or a few hours spent in the rooms of our American homes.

Most of the people in Belgium are early risers ; and if, by chance, you happen to visit any of her cities at dawn of day, you will find her churches full to overflowing with zealous Christians, who, like their time-honoured forefathers, offer the first fruits of the day to God, the giver of every good. The churches are numerous, large and beautiful, and multitudes of worshipers are in daily attendance. Men and women of the higher class attired in robes of broadcloth; poor peasant women, with little shawls or kerchiefs covering their heads and shoulders; blue-eyed, fair-faced children, and the aged; whose bent forms and tottering steps show that they are nearing the end of life's journey; all assemble in the early morning seeking mercy, peace and comfort at the Throne of Grace. We can imagine the effect of this morning's devotion, especially consoling to the poor, who, in their heavy *"blokken"* (wooden shoes) toil, day in and day out, all year long, for a small compensation, insufficient for the comfort of their families.

As are the parents, so are the children; particularly in the boarding-school, where the rules and regulations necessitate strict discipline. Shortly before or after five o'clock in the morning, every child is up, unless someone is ill, who, for the time, is excused from rising. After dressing, a sign is given and all descend in strict silence to the chapel for morning prayer and the holy sacrifice of the Mass. After morning devotions they go to the refectory, where a bounteous supply of *"botterham"* (bread and butter) and strong coffee is served. Breakfast is eaten in silence, except on special festivals.

Needless to say that a great amount of tact is necessary on the part of the monitor to keep one hundred little tongues within their ivory walls until the signal is given to go to the playground.

Here we found them at the beginning of our narrative; here we shall find them again at half-past nine, at twelve, after four-o'clock lunch, and after supper; in the summer evenings. In winter the time of recreation is spent in the reception hall of the boarding-school. At eight o'clock the school day ends, and all advance in strict silence to the dormitories to enjoy the peaceful slumber which health and youth affords.

The dormitories are four in number. Each child has a separate alcove. Several sisters are in attendance during the night. In case of illness, a child is immediately removed to another apartment.

To these general rules and regulations there are exceptions on Sundays and special festivals during the year. On those days special devotional exercises take place in the morning, the afternoon being assigned to the practicing of hymns and sacred music. When the weather is fine, the recesses are longer, and pleasant walks may be enjoyed in the garden. One Sunday in the month, called "Visiting Day," is at the disposal of parents and visitors, who are permitted to call upon the children.

CHAPTER 2

Daily School Life

Every Tuesday afternoon, from one until about four o'clock, all the boarders, except the little ones, dressed in full uniform, go forth for a long walk with their teachers. They usually visit churches, shrines, or places of particular interest, thus developing the spiritual, mental and physical powers of the body.

The uniform is quite becoming and attractive. It consists of a neat black dress, without showy trimmings or ornaments, black shoes and stockings, black hat, black silk gloves and necktie, with white sailor collar and cuffs. Sometimes white blouses, with straw hats, white silk neckties and gloves are worn. The hair is simply combed back, a part being taken up and fastened with a black or white bow, while the rest is braided and fastened again with a bow to match the necktie and gloves.

A silver chain, bearing the medal of the Immaculate Conception, is worn by all those belonging to the "Congregation of the Children of Mary."

For what might seem monotonous in this manner of dress, we find sufficient variation in the blond locks, naturally curling around the forehead, the plump, rosy cheeks, the sparkling eyes and smiling faces of these gay and guileless children.

The uniform is not permitted to be of costly fabric, as it must be in accordance with the means of every pupil. It is the distinguishing mark of the institution to which the child belongs, and claims for her a certain respect not due to those dressed in gaudy, striking, many-coloured garb, so often affected by girls and young ladies.

One of the principal and most beneficial results noticeable from the use of the uniform suit in the boarding-school is that it destroys the great inclination on the part of one pupil to surpass another in dress and personal adornment, thus preventing vanity and arrogance in the one, and removing the cause of envy, jealousy and distraction in the other.

What teacher has not remarked, in the ordinary classroom, the scornful glance on the face of a haughty child, as she regards her poorer neighbour's cheap dress, and who has not noticed the seeds of envy sprouting up in the heart of some poor little creature, so deeply wounded by the conduct of her affluent companion? There she sits, and, instead of diligently studying her lesson, that sensitive little soul is complaining against the All-Wise Providence, which has given to her neighbour more than to her. Alas! when that child returns home after school, poor mother must suffer. Her daughter begins to annoy and worry, tease and complain, until mother also feels the pangs of jealousy; and, falling into error, denies herself some household necessity in order to satisfy her discontented child. There are many mothers in the world at present who are real slaves to the caprices of their daughters in matters of dress. A pretty uniform in all common day schools would prevent a great deal of this annoyance to mothers, pupils and teachers.

Nearly every year since the opening of the sewing and household schools an exposition is held for about two weeks, in which all suits, lace, embroidery, painting, mending of clothing, and all other articles made by the boarders are exhibited.

Written invitations are sent out to the families and friends of the sisters and children. Only those who have received such invitations are allowed to visit the exposition.

It sometimes occurs that a dramatic performance is given by the boarders as an entertainment, wherein the play represents an event of particular religious or historical interest. In this case, also, only those invited are permitted to be present.

Most interesting entertainments, provided by the convent for the boarding-school, are the stereopticon views, with lectures given by the Reverend Professors of the College of Boom, in which are represented and discussed all the important scenes in and on the route to the Holy Land by those who have actually visited the scenes and secured the views themselves.

Another object of great interest is the *Play of the Birds*, presented by a French gentleman, when requested by the Superiors, for the pleasure and instruction of the pupils. There are several cages of birds of the smaller kinds. These birds are exactly trained, and, being perfectly obedient to their master, perform a series of exquisite feats, which leave a lasting impression on the memory. But the lesson which is intended to be impressed upon the minds of the pupils is the result which can be obtained from even the unreasoning creatures around us, by the unceasing, unwavering influence of a loving, gentle, patient and persevering character.

When the children had entered the classroom in the morning, the monitor stood for a moment and glanced around to see if the yard was in order. Her eye fell upon a paper forgotten by one of the pupils. She opened it and saw the portraits of the murdered crown prince and his noble consort, of Austria-Hungary, little recking the awful import of that heinous crime to her own fair country.

Was it the heat, or was it the harbinger of coming woe? A feeling of sadness so seldom experienced in the life of a zealous religious took possession of the Sister and carried her for the moment beyond her Convent walls, far away to the battlefield of life, where pride, ambition and materialism, like unto monstrous autocrats, wage war against the human race. A moment she pauses while her heart exclaims, "*Sursum Corda*" (Lift up the hearts).

One day in Thy house, O Lord, is better than thousands in the dwellings of sinners.

She glanced around the yard and went slowly to her room.

From the window could be seen the sunny, cloudless sky, the trees laden with ripening fruit, and far away those fertile, well-tilled fields in which, perhaps, there never had been raised before, a more plentiful or luxuriant crop of wheat and barley. Who could have ever thought that within a few short weeks that same, sunny sky would be raining death-dealing bombs upon the innocent inhabitants of a peace-loving nation, while her crops, over-ripe for the harvest, were being trampled under foot and her plains and meadows deluged in a sea of blood?

How strange, how incomprehensible does it not appear to those whose lives are spent in the abode of sanctity, to witness this ignoble strife, this worship of mammon, the rise and fall of the victims of ambition, along the path of glory leading to the grave? All the wealth of the world cannot obtain for them the precious pearl of peace, or the tranquillity of mind possessed by the poorest day labourer in the humble performance of his allotted task.

Peace is a hidden manna, unknown to the selfish lover of the world, in whose heart rages perpetual war.

On the outer page of a child's copy book, I observed an illustration which depicted in a very simple manner the progress of selfish ambition as it is found today in every class of society. In the corner of the page sat a big black spider, intent on catching a little fly which had lit on a blade of grass. Just above was a greedy little bird, ready to grasp the spider. At a short distance a vicious-looking old cat crouched in the grass, ready to spring at the bird. A dog, prowling along the street, seeing the cat, showed his long teeth and would have sprung at the cat, had not a little boy approached and begun to worry the dog. In the distance appears father, with the "rod of correction" in hand, ready to punish little Fritz for cruelty to animals.

Thus there is selfish strife in this world of ours, strife from the cradle to the grave; and no one, however proud, ambitious or arrogant he may be, who will not, one day, find a master greater than he. Now what is the object of this never-ending strife? It is simply an insatiable desire for superiority and self-satisfaction, even if, to obtain the ends in view, one must trample upon the rights of others.

Having lost original happiness in the fall of Adam, man has been looking for it ever since; but the great trouble is that many people look for it in the wrong direction, and seek it where no happiness is to be found. They think it consists in the acquisition of fame and glory, in the possession of wealth, or in a life of ease and luxury; but these things are as transient as the evening twilight, and uncertain as the shadowy forms portrayed in the river's depths. The entire lives of many people are consumed in a fruitless search after the vain and perishable goods of the earth. Their years glide away like the sands in an hour-glass; and, finally they sicken, faint and fall, and their end resembles the pebbles thrown into the ocean, which for a moment ripple the surface and lose themselves in its waves. The human soul is as a fathomless sea, which nothing finite can satisfy. "*O God!*" cried St. Augustine, "*Thou hast made us for Thyself, and our hearts are ever troubled, ever agitated, until they find rest in Thee.*"

CHAPTER 3

The Parochial School, Convent and Garden

The reverie into which the sister had fallen was soon interrupted by the sound of children's voices in the small playground. Hastily leaving the room, she went to meet the merry little band of day-scholars who attend the boarding-school from half-past eight in the morning until six o'clock in the evening.

Joyfully the little group of twenty gathers around their mistress. One presents a flower which mother had given; another, a pretty postcard; yet another shows a toy or picture-book. A chubby little boy is crying because he has forgotten his new drum; and thus talking, laughing and crying, they are placed in line and lead away to the cosy little classroom whose long, broad windows look out upon the garden, which is ever green, and the rose bushes near the arbour, which bloom the greater part of the year, and on whose twigs buds were often seen on New Year's Day.

During the morning session one rosy-cheeked little girl, with long yellow curls and an apron as white as snow, stood up by her desk and said, "Sister, there is war in the newspapers. Papa said so this morning." All the little heads turned, curious to hear about the war; and little Charlie took out his box of soldiers and arranged them in marching order on the desk. The mistress took advantage of the situation to teach the older pupils the great value of peace and the reward promised to the peacemakers *"Blessed are the peacemakers, for they shall be called the children of God."*

At half-past nine the recess bell rings, and all the pupils proceed once more to the playground and play tag, or continue their needlework in the shade of the wide-spreading trees. During certain seasons of the year all children play "beads," which is quite similar to a game of marbles. Happier than a general returning with the spoils of war is the child who, at the end of the season, can show her companions a string of large, many-coloured beads two or three yards long.

The swing and the rings are the source of great enjoyment for the children, and not a little care and anxiety to the Sister on guard, especially if the ripening fruit hangs on a branch within touching range of the children's feet.

When it freezes hard in the winter, there being no snow on the ground and no pond nearer than the large garden, a number of the older pupils pump water and throw it on the stone pavement of the playground, until the whole becomes as a sheet of glass; and then the exercise of skating on wooden shoes begins. Needless to say, there is danger of fracturing more than the pavement when this play begins.

Sister M. Anastatia has been for about twenty-eight years *preceptress* in the boarding-school. She is a small, slight figure, whose very presence has a kind of magic influence upon all around her. At her entrance and during her lessons perfect order prevails. Authority and precision, softened by great kindness of heart, are the distinctive personal traits of Sister M. Anastatia. She is assisted in her work by several other sisters and two lady teachers.

Among the assistants, no one, perhaps, deserves more credit or gratitude than Sister M. Cecilia, who for more than twenty-five years has directed the musical exercises of the convent and boarding-school.

Showing a natural talent for music in her early childhood, and possessing a fine voice, her own progress in this art has been remarkable, and her services inestimable as teacher of music and directress of the choir. She is assisted in her work by Sister M. Margarita, one of the younger sisters of the community.

The Belgians, like many other European nations, are great lovers of music. Thus, since a large number of pupils take music lessons, the monotony of school life is broken by the melody of many instruments and the sweet harmony of children's voices.

There is no place where the influence of soft, sweet music is so effective as in the church or chapel during devotional exercises. Nowhere are greater pains taken to develop this art as a branch of education than in the convent schools, and nowhere are the results obtained more gratifying.

Sister M. Amelia, the only child of the well-known family Le Duc, of Mechelen, entered the convent at the age of sixteen, and having completed the normal course in St. Nicholas, took charge of one of the higher departments in the boarding-school. She teaches French and Flemish, also drawing, painting and penmanship. The English and German languages are taught in the higher departments.

Proceeding from the boarding-school, the visitor is led around to the long playground of the Parochial School of Willebroeck. Here between six and seven hundred girls form the long line which is marching through the gate of "*d'Externat.*" Each division is in charge of one or more sisters, who conduct the children safely through the street a little beyond the Post-office. Here the procession breaks up, and the children scatter in all directions and run on to their homes in the different parts of the town.

Scarcely have the sisters finished dinner, when the throng of pupils are at the gate again, eager for admittance. See them coming from all directions, and listen to the clatter of their wooden shoes on the stone pavement. Truly happy in their child-like simplicity, strong, healthy and active, they are worthy descendants of a sturdy old race. When the gate is opened, crowds rush into the yard and begin their games of tag, jump the rope, hide and seek, etc., just as easily in those hard "*blokken*" as their next-door neighbours, the "*pensionnaires*" (boarders), in fine high-heeled shoes.

The continual use of wooden shoes is hurtful to the feet. They hinder the development of natural gracefulness in walking and cause the feet to become large and very flat

Sister M. Stanislas superintends the Parochial School. Though small of stature and very delicate, she has worked for years in the cause of education and has become one of the most prominent teachers in the province. In company with her associates, the assistant teachers, she attends the conferences, writes articles on education and conference work, directs the sewing department; in a word, it is greatly due to her zeal, energy and Christian charity that the Girls' Catholic School of Willebroeck has attained as high a standing as the highly paid public schools of the district.

On leaving "*d'Externat*" (parochial school) one enters that part of the garden especially assigned to the use of the sisters during recreation. It adjoins the large garden which is at the service of strangers on Sundays and visiting days. From the main path, in the middle of the garden, a fine view can be had of that quaint old convent, some of whose buildings have stood there over a hundred years. On the right rises the new school, containing several large classrooms on one side; and on the other, the bakery, laundry, free sewing and household schools. At a short distance from the school is the "*gloriette*" (arbour), or summer house, surrounded by a very beautiful collection of rose bushes, then in full bloom. There are beds also containing many varieties of flowers, palms and evergreens.

In the distance is seen the convent chapel, with its small belfry. It seems so insignificant in comparison with the majestic tower of the old parish church of Willebroeck, which, probably, has weathered the storms of centuries.

On the right-hand side of the chapel is found the "Grotto," or Shrine of Our Blessed Lady of Lourdes." It is here that the children, during the summer evenings, sing their sweetest hymns; here also that the Sisters, after a tiresome day's work, kneel in spirit a few moments at the feet of their "Holy Mother" and patroness, who gave to the world the first perfect model of Convent life, when as a child she parted with her dearly beloved parents, St. Joachim and St. Anna, and entered the Temple of Jerusalem, where the years of her childhood were passed in work, in prayer, and in devout communion with the Divine Being, who was "Lord of the Temple."

The number of religious now, (1916), in the convent is fifty. They are Sisters of the Augustinian Order, bearing the name of *Filles de Marie* (Daughters of Mary). The Mother House, wherein reside the Superior General, Rev. Mother M. Berchmans, and Assistant Superior, Rev. Sister M. Gabrielle, is, and has been for about fifty years, in the town of Willebroeck, in the Province of Antwerp, Belgium.

In this house all the younger sisters are received, trained, and make their profession, which consists in the solemn pronunciation of the three holy vows of religion.

Many of the younger sisters complete their normal course for .school teachers during their novitiate.

The mission houses arc Thisselt, Blaesvelt, Aertselaar and Bonheyden. All the sisters are Belgians, except one.

During the last eighteen years five of the members have celebrated the golden jubilee, or fiftieth anniversary of their entrance into the Community. One of these. Rev. Mother M. Magdalena, was the sister of the late well-known and highly esteemed Bishop of Richmond, Va., Rt Rev. A. Van de Vyver, D. D. She entered at the age of eighteen and lived fifty-seven years in the convent.

We stood by the death-bed of all these dear old members who had given the flower and fruit of their long and useful lives to the advance of education and religion. We observed the peaceful resignation on the countenance of each dying sister, and the smile of heavenly joy on her lips. The death of each one of these was for the Community as the passing away of a sunbeam. For them it was only a happy transition from the sorrows of time to the joys of eternity. We gazed on those faces so pure, so calm, so majestic, even after the spirit had fled, and recalled the words of Holy Scripture, "*Blessed are the dead who die in the Lord,*" and again, "*The death of the just is precious in the sight of the Lord.*"

Besides the above named, there are a number of sisters in the convent who have already celebrated their "Silver Jubilee," or twenty-fifth anniversary of their entrance.

Under the administration of the so-called Liberal party in Belgium, in the year 1879, the Catholic schools, being deprived of financial assistance from the government, were closed.

A new School Law was passed, and the Crucifix and images of the saints were prohibited in the schools. Many Catholic teachers resigned. The clergy and rich Catholic families built schools of their own, which were supported by gifts.

Our community provided schools for the poor children of Willebroeck, and furnished the classrooms with desks, books and all necessary supplies. The eight sisters who taught received only 2,000 *francs* per year, which was less than fifty dollars for each Sister, and the predicament of the Sisters became more or less alarming. Several prominent gentlemen in the town, among whom was Mr. Erix, the father of our present Sister M. Aloisia, went around taking up collections for the pressing necessities of the community.

In the year 1866, when the cholera broke out in Willebroeck, three sisters went to the hospital; and, without any compensation whatever, remained with their patients. Later, about the year 1891, the same disease broke out again. The Liberal *burgomaster*, Mr. De Naeyer, being in great need of assistance, came to the convent and asked for sisters as nurses. Regardless of their past grievances, occasioned by the bitter opposition of the Liberals to the Catholic schools, eager only to do good, five strong, able-bodied sisters, at the request of their Superior, left the convent and went to the temporary hospital which had been hastily erected in the town.

Here they remained day and night, in the midst of death and disease, at the bedside of their stricken fellow-creatures until the epidemic ceased. Strange to say, not one of the sisters contracted the disease, although numbers of their patients died each day.

Only two of those heroines of charity and self-sacrifice now, (1916), survive: Sister M. Theresia and Sister M. Perpetua. These two sisters, feeble and aged, were obliged to take flight into Holland last September, but have now returned, with several others, to their convent home in Willebroeck.

CHAPTER 4

The Cloister

Proceeding from the little Grotto of Lourdes, where the sisters kneel in the evening for their "*Drie Wees Gegroeten*" (three Hail Marys), one passes through the large, stone-paved playground, over the small yard, and enters the corridor leading to the Chapel.

Passing through the yard, we observe the Novitiate on the left. This may be considered the preparatory school of religious life. Here no one is received under the age of twenty-one, without full consent of parents or guardians. Immediately a regular course of training begins, in which the duties and obligations of religious life are clearly presented. No applicant is permitted to take the vows who has not voluntarily responded to the requirements of the novitiate.

Before taking the vows, every postulant, if not satisfied, is perfectly free to return to her own home. Thus the obligations which bind one to religious life are not incurred by entering a convent or taking the veil, as some people suppose, but by the solemn and voluntary pronunciation of the vows, which in our community may not take place without special dispensation, in less than a year after receiving the habit. In the novitiate a Training Class has been established for those who intend to teach school. If not already graduates, this course is usually followed by the novice, who later enters the Normal School.

The experiences of the novitiate make a life-long impression on the mind, and are regarded by the religious of more mature years as the scenes of childhood in the home circle are looked upon by the people of the world.

On the right of the hall is seen the large folding door leading to the community room of the sisters. This apartment, especially devoted to the private use of the "professed members," is never entered by the worldling, except with special permission from higher authority, and then only in case of necessity, as, for instance, a workman, for necessary repairs.

Enter then in spirit this earthly paradise and try, if possible, to comprehend the charm which permeates it. Here we meet rich and poor, old and young. They call each other "Sister." They greet in passing with these words, "*Geloof d Zij Jezus Christus*" (Praised Be Jesus Christ), to atone for the profane use of the sacred Name by the vulgar.

The sisters are all dressed alike; thus, no vain love of dress, no envy, no jealousy. They lose no precious time at the dressing table, and no money is wasted in following the vagaries and follies of every changing season. Their food is the same (exceptions being made for the sick and feeble) , simple and substantial, neither rich nor dainty. The result is, as a rule, a measure of health and physical strength unknown in the circles of society.

The rules and regulations to which they voluntarily subject themselves relieve them of all care and encumbrance as to the future. Each member performs her work as faithfully and diligently as possible; and the good "All Father" provides. They join each other in prayer and in the recreation. They assist each other in pain, in sickness and sorrow, and comfort one another in the hour of death.

The work of the members is not the same. Each has a special office or work to perform.

As the different organs of the body cooperate in preserving life, and even the smallest screw in the locomotive is necessary to the accomplishment of its work, so does each member contribute to the spiritual life and well-being of the community.

From this place is banished all that makes life miserable for millions of people. That is, particularly, the great desire of worldly possession—having, ever having, and never having enough—also, the ever-increasing desire and search for pleasure, pastime and self-satisfaction; but finding only pain, chagrin and remorse; that is, finally, the insatiable desire for freedom from all bonds and fetters which sanctify the soul and keep the body in restraint; and while thus seeking liberty, one finds, as a rule, in himself a most cruel tyrant for matter.

The sisters retire at an appointed hour and arise at the first sound of the bell. They work faithfully and industriously all day long, all year long, all their lives.

Their wages are neither gold nor silver. They are the eternal merits which they know awaits them in a better life. The false and artificial customs of the world are strangers here. This short and sorrowful life is looked upon as a pilgrimage in a land of exile, or as the passage of a train from which the traveller joyfully observes the fleeting objects along the route, well knowing that every disappearing mile-post reduces the distance between him and his dearly beloved home.

The sisterhood is as a garden of many flowers, where the pure white lily never loses its beauty, where the red rose of love has made place for the pure white blossom of Christian Charity; and the fragrant little violet of humility diffuses incense to the angels who ascend and descend about the Throne of God.

People often condole the religious closed up within the prison walls of the convent and forever deprived of the joys and pleasures of the world. Little they know that within these same walls the heart is as free as the flight of the bird, while the soul in solitude is in constant communion with God, whose Divine Presence is felt in the life that surrounds her.

She hears His voice in the gentle sigh of the breeze, in the hum of the bee, in the song of the bird and in the soft murmur of the little brooklet breaking over the mountainside. His wonderful attributes become visible to a certain degree in every object around her. She admires His Divine Providence in the fatherly care which He takes of His creatures. Even the tiniest insect and the smallest blade of grass show forth the love, wisdom and the goodness of God.

The soul in solitude, hidden within the convent walls, admires the grandeur and glory of God as manifested in the majestic rising and setting of the sun, and its influence over all nature. God's beauty is seen in the colour of the clouds and in the ever-varying tints of the sky. The fragrance of the flowers reminds her of the odour of sanctity which a Christian should leave in his wake; and if, as sometimes occurs, one observes anything which mars the beautiful face of Nature or disturbs the peaceful course of events, it brings to mind the revolting sight of a soul in sin and the remorse and confusion it must suffer.

The wave on the ocean's breast; those giant rocks on the shore; the mountains and little hills; the river flowing on to the sea; the moss and ferns in the wood; in a word, every object in and around proclaim to the religious the omnipotence and omnipresence of Him who created them.

The soul detached from the temporal, and seeking only the eternal, forsakes the creature to find the Creator; and, having found Him, has found what her heart desired.

What are, then, the pleasures of earth to those who have tasted the sweetness of Grace; more delicious than the luxuries of a thousand worlds? They speak no more of the past, since for them a new and happier life has begun. With eyes and hearts fixed on heaven, they have forgotten the earth and, enraptured cry out;

Laetatus sum in his qui dicta sunt mihi; in domum domini ibimus. (I was rejoiced at those things which were said to me: We shall go into the house of the Lord.)

CHAPTER 5

The Approaching Storm

July's sun sank gently away on the western horizon, and its last rays lit up the ripening fruit, the plants and flowers in the garden. It seemed to linger for a last farewell to the groups of merry children who, unconscious of their fast-approaching woe, were cheerfully singing Belgium's well-known national song, "The Proud Flemish Lion."

In a few moments the "Golden Gate" closed on a field of purple haze, shutting out that blessed glimpse of heaven, while the black shroud of the most dismal night in history darkened the sky of that hapless nation.

The sisters were together in the evening recreation of that fateful day, when word was received that King Albert of Belgium, in order to fulfil his obligations of neutrality, had refused the *kaiser's* army access to his territory to attack the French. Had a thunderbolt fallen from a clear sky, or an earthquake shaken the ground under foot, it would scarcely have surprised or terrorised the people more than did the *kaiser's* declaration of war against this free and happy little kingdom.

When hostilities broke out between Austria and Servia, while realising the possibility of trouble in the country in case of a general war, we were assured that Belgium, being a neutral nation and having no other desire than that of possessing her own soil, and living in peace with all nations, had nothing to fear from war or invasion.

Feeble human insight into the designs of Providence, whose hand has the power to destroy and rebuild, to crown or dethrone kings and *kaisers*, and seal the fate of nations.

It is not our object to discuss the causes of the European war from a material point of view, nor do we intend to pass judgment upon the nations or individuals engaged in it; nevertheless, viewing the present condition of affairs in Europe from another standpoint, and drawing conclusions from observation and personal experience, we must admit that a spiritual warfare had been raging there for several years.

Certainly, God, who is the source of peace, virtue and every good, should have been permitted to hold sovereign sway in His own kingdom; that is, in the hearts of His children and in the homesteads of His people. This right was disregarded in a most ruthless manner for many years, as is evident from the fact that the word "*God*" and everything pertaining to God, was expunged from the text-books in some places in Europe, while it would have been a serious offense for a teacher to mention His sacred name or anything in connection therewith in the classroom.

The spirit of atheism and agnosticism contended against the Spirit of Religion, and as a scourging wind was fast sweeping over the land, leaving by the wayside thousands of incautious souls bereft of all ennobling possessions of mind and heart.

The vices and vanities of pagan Rome were reviving before our very eyes in about the same manner as they had been prevalent over twenty hundred years ago; and, although idolatrous shrines were not found in the homesteads, they could easily be found in the hearts of many people.

Modern life in Europe, especially in the large cities, had to a certain degree, lost its high ideal of perfection, as did the world in the time of Noah; and, consequently, it does not seem indiscreet to intimate that the same Supremacy which chastised the world in the great flood, has, for the same reason, reappeared and become manifest in the deluge of blood which now inundates the soil of those unhappy nations.

Civilization, wealth, industry and intellect developed in times of peace and prosperity, so as to reach apparently the limit of effort, have exhausted their entire resources up to this time to construct means suitable for destroying themselves.

Now the question has been asked, "Why could not Christianity, after a period of about twenty hundred years on earth, have prevented this cruel war and saved the honour of civilization?" The answer is not difficult to find. Christianity could and would have saved humanity from this dreadful misfortune had it not been for the fact that her power had been checked, her authority limited, her work hindered and her ranks weakened by those heavy storms which, though unable to uproot the Divine Institution, have impeded her progress and lessened her influence over the human race. When the happy day dawns in which the true spirit of Christianity, free and unfettered, will animate civilization as the soul animates the body, then, and not till then, will its powerful influence be able to dispel the shades of darkness in the minds of men, and in the palaces of kings and *kaisers*. Then will war cease and the reign of peace and happiness begin.

CHAPTER 6

Changes

When our minds, bewildered by the unexpected course which affairs had taken, fully comprehended that the country was at war, a feeling of dismay and terror, never before experienced, took possession of all.

Suitable measures were adopted for the safety of the children under our care, to whom the usual prizes were distributed on the first Sunday in August, a week before the ordinary time of vacation. Permission was also given them to return to their homes the following day. All necessary preparations were made as quickly as possible, and early next morning the boarders, accompanied by one or more sisters, departed in groups to their homes in the surrounding cities and towns.

The parochial and public schools of the village continued in session for a few days, as the children were all residents, and no immediate danger was anticipated.

Subsequently, while the train containing a party of our pupils *en route* for Mechelen (Malines) was steaming on at full speed, it was hailed by a troop of Belgian soldiers, and instantly slackened up. All passengers were obliged to alight and, with satchels and small baggage in hand, had to make their way to the city as best they could, a walk of an hour or more. The soldiers boarded the train, which immediately started off to another station.

At home the general cleaning and arrangement of the boarding-school began, and in a few days the united assistance of strong hands and willing hearts have accomplished the work, and the sisters quietly await developments.

During this time several workmen were busy excavating a cellar in the yard. On a certain morning the implements remained idly standing by the wall, as the workmen had been called out to assist in the all-important work of strengthening the fortification of Willebroeck. This cellar, half filled with water by the dislodgment of the pipes leading to the cisterns, became later the receptacle of the bomb which passed through the chapel, shattering the walls and windows in its course.

One night a great noise in the streets aroused the residents of Willebroeck. It was the call for several classes of soldiers who were obliged to rise, pack their kits and depart in a few hours, perhaps never more to return to their homes or families. Sorrow filled many a homestead that morning, but it was only a faint shadow of what was yet to come.

Shortly afterwards it was announced that all the horses were to be brought to the public market-place in each city and village. Here they were examined and those unfit rejected. We know not whether any compensation was given to the owners at this time, although promise was made to make good the loss sustained at the close of the war. All the horses which could be of any service had to be given up for the use of the army. There were some people who gave seven, some nine, and one, we knew, who gave thirteen or fourteen. Thus, just about the time that the harvest was ripe in the fields, men and horses had to leave home and go to meet death on the field of battle.

Imagine the plight of women and children, with every kind of hard work on hand and no one to help. How happy they were when, as happened occasionally, their poor old horses were rejected by the officers. Shortly thereafter all the bicycles and motor cars had to be delivered, and yet neither complaint nor murmur was heard on the part of the people, who patiently resigned themselves to the unhappy lot which had befallen them.

The gazettes and daily papers were eagerly read, although little reliable information could be obtained. Encouraging news in the evening was usually contradicted in the morning, while reports of the most terrible atrocities; of men murdered in cold blood; of open and gross lawlessness and evil conduct, terrorised the peaceful population in the unprotected towns and villages.

Shortly after the war began letters were received from His Eminence, Card. Mercier, Archbishop of Malines, requesting the use of the schools and other locales for a military hospital to be placed at the service of the Red Cross.

Again a few days of quiet anticipation elapse, like the calm which precedes a destructive storm; while the sisters utilise the time in the unusual occupation of changing the joyful abode of children into a fit dwelling for death and misery.

The children's refectory was arranged for the care of wounded officers; the large reception hall was fitted up for wounded soldiers, also the three dormitories and several classrooms. One classroom became an office for chaplain and doctors. Another department became an operating room. Another was reserved for cases of contagious disease which might occur, while another room was used as a mortuary.

One Sunday morning, about the middle of August, an unusual tumult was heard on the street. The door bell was loudly rung, and a messenger admitted with news that the officers of the Belgian War Department had commanded everything within firing range of the fortress to be cleared away at once. For some time previous the soldiers had been busy cutting down the groves and all the trees in the immediate vicinity of the fortress. The poor people were given just three hours to get away with bag and baggage.

Willebroeck, a large village between Antwerp and Brussels, about two miles from the City of Boom, had increased greatly in population, wealth and manufacturing during the years of peace and prosperity which had elapsed since the last war. Thus it happened that stores, dwelling houses, farm houses, breweries, paper mills and other industries had been built up, regardless of the fortification near by, whose grass-covered walls concealed the strong masonry and heavy cannon within.

This was a terrible misfortune for about six hundred families, whose dwellings, being located within the limits prescribed, had to be levelled to the ground. Even the tombstones in the cemetery, together with all the crops, trees, haystacks, barns and everything within range of the gaping mouths of the cannon, had to be laid flat or taken away.

No wonder that the people raced to and fro that hot Sunday morning, carrying bundles, dragging wagons with household furniture and fixtures; wheeling trunks, clothing, stoves, pictures, bedding and every article that could be taken up and carried away. Tears and perspiration rolled over the cheeks of men and women, whose faces glowed from the heat and intense excitement

Fortunately, the first message was followed by another whereby the people were allowed more time to get their personal property in safety before the work of "burning off" began. Impossible to describe how bitterly hard it was for these poor people to tear themselves away from the homes which had cost them so much toil, labour and hardship.

The new Sewing School and laundry, the Parochial School, the Girls' Public School, the Patronage (Boys' Catholic School), and all other large locales received the village refugees. In a short time cows, horses, chickens, coal, grain, vegetables, furniture and everything that one can well imagine filled up the schools and gardens. The cattle, unused to the change and flurry, set up a dreadful howling, which continued long into the night

In one schoolroom we had the contents of a grocery store; in another the costly furniture of one of the richest gentlemen in the town; while several families took up their abode in the midst of the clothing, furniture and bedding in the schools. How we all worked that day, carrying out desks and piling them up in safe places, putting away books, school utensils—as many as possible in the least possible space. Every available spot on the ground was utilized, except those rooms assigned to the private use of the sisters, and the boarding-school, which was reserved for the use of the Red Cross.

The poor people resigned themselves to these changes without complaint or murmur; and the sisters, notwithstanding the disorder and confusion caused by this state of affairs, did all that was possible to assist and make them comfortable.

CHAPTER 7

War

It is only when a common calamity, such as this, threatens not only the happiness, but also the very existence, of a whole nation, and the inundating tide of misfortune rises to the very doors of rich and poor, that the fountains of true Christian Charity spring open and lave with refreshing draughts the parched lips of the afflicted. The same burden that one bears on his shoulder is borne in the heart of another, who, while alleviating the wants of his neighbour, must think of his own approaching ruin.

In such moments, while the seal of humble submission is stamped on the sorrow-stricken heart of suffering humanity, the haughty arrogance of creatures recedes before that resistless Power which shapes the destinies of men and nations, despite the best-laid plans and precautions.

The work of "burning off" the houses did not proceed rapidly enough, as the walls were of stone, and the roofs of tile or slate, and much of the wooden furniture had been removed, so pulleys, brought into action by electricity, were adjusted to the walls, and thus these houses, so dear to the hearts of the people, were actually pulled over upon the ground. Whole streets had to be levelled and all the residents left without a shelter. Many of these did not possess the means of providing other homes. However, the firm hope of final victory and the restoration of their lost property sustained them in this dark and dreary hour.

In the meantime a most terrible battle was taking place at the fortification of Liege. Was ever attack so strong, or resistance more determined? Belgian officers said "The enemy were twenty to one against us; but, being obliged to face the terrible fires of the fortress, their ranks were cut down in about the same manner as wheat it cut off by the reaper." "So great was the number of the Germans that they seemed to spring up out of the ground." "They crawled ahead on hands and feet, and at a given signal sprang erect and fired, and then again prostrated themselves. Thus they advanced, avoiding as much as possible the heavy fires in front." Another Belgian officer at the fortress during the battle said: "It resembled a storm of fiery hailstones from a cloud of smoke, in an atmosphere suffocating with heat and the smell of powder."

Eyewitnesses relate that heaps of slain, yards high, were found on the battlefield, while columns of lifeless bodies were observed in a standing position, there being no place for the dead to fall.

A story was told by one of the Belgian officers of a German soldier who, when wounded by a Belgian in a hand-to-hand combat, took out a coin and presented it. The Belgian, surprised, exclaimed "*Zijt gij zot?*" (Are you crazy?) "Do you not know that I've broken your arm?"

"Yes," said the German, "This is to show my gratitude for the favour you've rendered me, since it gives me the opportunity of leaving the battlefield."

Much was said about the valour of the soldiers on both sides during the siege of Liege. The Germans were obliged to advance in the face of destructive fires. If one should retreat, he would be pierced by the bayonet of the soldier behind him.

Certain it is, whether we observe the Germans as friends or foes, all must admit that their courage, endurance and military tactics have surprised the whole world.

Sad it is to think that such manhood, intelligence and bravery is not trained to love the conquests of peace.

The Belgians, far inferior in number, fought with a valour which clearly shows the undying love of country and of freedom which has ever been a distinguishing characteristic of this noble-minded race.

It is not the first time that her fields have been deluged with the blood of her heroes, in whose honour and memory we find, in the flag of Belgium, beside the yellow, which signifies the kingdom, a red stripe to remind her people of the blood shed for freedom, and a black stripe in mourning for her slain.

While facing death in this first great battle at the fortress of Liege, one of the soldiers began to sing the well-known national hymn, "The Proud Flemish Lion." Immediately the strains were taken up by the whole regiment, and thus singing, they advanced until hundreds of them fell in that awful conflict.

In the heaviest of the fray we were told that King Albert had placed himself in the lines with his soldiers. He did not desire to be called king, but comrade. His military dress was distinguished from the others by only a small mark on one of the sleeves. He attended to the correspondence for his soldiers and was regarded by them as a friend and father, under whose guidance they were ready to fight and die.

When the siege was over he visited the wounded in many of the hospitals and addressed each soldier in person.

As I remember, the siege of Liege lasted about two weeks. Finally, the strong walls of the fortress began to give way, thus demonstrating the uselessness of the old-time means of protection when obliged to withstand the shells and bombs of modern siege guns.

The German officers themselves praised the valour of the Belgians. We were told that the German commander refused to accept the sword from the Belgian officer, unwilling to submit the latter to this humiliation, since it was not for want of valour or through any fault of his that the fort had to be surrendered, but on account of the superior forces of the enemy and the all-destroying power of his heavy siege guns, some of which were said to shoot a distance of nearly thirty miles.

Needless to dwell upon the horrors which took place throughout the length and breadth of the country after the entrance of the enormous army of the Germans, whose plans had been so unexpectedly frustrated by the determined resistance of the Belgians.

These fought long and valiantly in expectation of assistance from the Allies, who, unprepared for the sudden progress of the campaign, were unable to render the necessary assistance in the beginning of the war. This is the explanation which was given by both the French and English as to the tardiness in the arrival of the help expected from those countries.

After the fall of Liege, when the enemy entered the city, the Rt Rev. Bishop of the diocese, the *burgomaster* of the city and several others of the more prominent residents were taken prisoners as hostages. These, as a rule, are put to death if the requirements of the enemy be not exactly met.

Sometime later we heard that these hostages were set at liberty.

Then followed the destruction of many cities, towns and villages along the route, including the noted City of Louvain, the heart of Catholic Belgium, the principal place of her Christian educational institutions, and the seat of her missionary forces.

Consternation filled the minds of the Belgians at the needless destruction of this ancient city, with its treasures of art and sculpture, its schools, colleges, libraries, and particularly its world-renowned university.

CHAPTER 8

The Carnage of Battle

After the fall of Liege and Namur, the destruction of Louvain and a number of noted cities, towns and villages, our minds were concerned with that awe-inspiring event—the advance of the enemy to Brussels.

Well do we remember that beautiful summer evening, when our prayers and evening meditation in the chapel were disturbed for about an hour by the continuous whirl of automobiles passing the convent. We were told that evening that it was the departure of the legislative body from Brussels to Antwerp, with the archives and treasures of the government.

Our hearts seemed to grow cold and leaden within us as we sat there hoping, praying, fearing, yet instinctively feeling the doom so rapidly approaching.

One gloomy, rainy day, word came that over two thousand soldiers of the Civil Guard had lowered their weapons at the approach of the enemy and quietly surrendered the City of Brussels, Belgium's beautiful capital. To have fought without fortifications against such superior forces as the Germans possessed would have been a useless sacrifice of life.

Strict, in the extreme, were the regulations enforced by the Germans in the different places which they entered. They also levied enormous war taxes. Bold and undaunted even to the verge of imprudence, as was then remarked by the Belgians, was the conduct of Burgomaster Max, of Brussels, in his conduct toward the enemy.

The work of strengthening and completing the fortification of Willebroeck, said to be amongst the strongest in the world, continued, while a large number of soldiers, as watch guards, were constantly on duty.

The electricity which supplied light to the village and kept many a motor propelling, was entirely cut off from the houses and public buildings and concentrated at the fort.

Two thousand workmen engaged in the paper factories of Mr. Louis De Naeyer were out of work. Charitable ladies, aided by Madame De Naeyer, of the Castle of Willebroeck, and assisted in the work by some of the sisters, met daily at the Boys' Public School and made ready a good, strong soup, which was dealt out in cans or pitchers to the destitute families of these poor workmen.

The paper factories, the Castle of Blaesvelt, belonging to a former Belgian Ambassador to Washington, whose wife was a native of that city, and the large and newly equipped breweries of the Erix families, were stripped of their machinery and made to serve as fortresses by boring holes through their walls for the reception of cannon and *mettrailleusen* (machine guns). The paper factory itself, commanding a good position near the bridge of the canal, was so arranged that it could be flooded at a moment's warning; and this was actually done, as we were informed by the refugees in England, when the battle at the fortress took place prior to the fall of Antwerp.

During the progress of the campaign in the vicinity at that time, several occurrences affected, in a great measure, every aspect of daily life for the quiet residents of Willebroeck, and particularly for the Sisters, unaccustomed as they were to any participation in the affairs of the world, except such as were imperative for the direction and maintenance of their schools.

These were: First, the arrival of the Red Cross and wounded soldiers, some six weeks before our departure from Antwerp; second, the return of the army; third, the flight of the refugees; fourth, the daily increasing and ever nearer approaching roar of the cannonade.

One afternoon in the middle of August a large, heavy wagon was drawn into the yard. It bore the flag of the Red Cross on top, and on the side in great white letters the words "Military Hospital."

In a few minutes a fleshy little gentleman, who at once distinguished himself as the "*chef*" (chief), and a number of other gentlemen, about thirty-five in all, wearing white bands with red crosses on their arms, and long white linen coats over their uniforms, such as bakers sometimes wear, were seen hurrying to and fro, unpacking and carrying their various instruments and utensils to the operating room.

A military chaplain and four or more doctors accompanied the group. All except the chaplain were dressed in uniform. Several young ladies of Willebroeck, former members of our Boarding-school, dressed in white and wearing the head-dress and armband of the Red Cross, came next day and graciously presented themselves to aid in taking care of the wounded.

The services rendered by the Red Cross in time of war is simply inestimable. "When circumstances permit, there are three different posts or places where the wounded are treated," said the village doctor who assisted in training the young lady volunteers to the Red Cross army. "The first post is only a few yards distant from the battlefield and as near as possible to the firing line. This post is very dangerous. Only volunteers are sent there, as a rule. The members go out on the field in search of the wounded, amid the continual bursting of partially exploded shells. One careless step may cause serious wounds or instant death. Then again, after a battle has been fought, there is occasional shooting, even in the night; but the members of the Red Cross have consecrated themselves to the service of the sick and wounded soldiers, and God gives them strength and courage according to their necessities."

When found, the wounded are brought into the first post on stretchers or in ambulance wagons, and only those attentions which are absolutely necessary are given. Then they are taken to the second post or hospital, where a more thorough examination takes place and the necessary operations are performed, which consist principally in the extraction of bullets, setting and amputation of broken limbs, etc.

Here they remain until they become convalescent, unless the number of wounded soldiers increases to such a degree as to prevent proper care being taken of them, in which case they are taken away to a third hospital, where they are supposed to remain until their wounds are entirely healed. Then they ardently desire, if not maimed, to return again to the front

When a seriously wounded soldier is brought into the hospital, he is stripped of his clothing, wrapped in a sheet and carried to the operating room. This service is rendered by the gentlemen of the Red Cross. One or more of the lady nurses assist at the operation. If the soldier is mortally wounded and there is apprehension of immediate dissolution, he remains in the sheets and is lovingly cared for by these gentlemen until death occurs. Then the body is rolled in the sheet, placed in a coffin and buried the next day.

Coffins were provided by our village for the soldiers who died in our hospital. One day nine were carried away to the cemetery; another day, two; then one or two. Several were dead or at the point of death when they were brought into the hospital.

One poor factory woman came inquiring for her husband. We did not dare tell her that he died immediately when brought in, but left this sad task for Rev. Mother Superior.

On another day a woman and her daughter-in-law came from a great distance inquiring for her son, the young woman's husband. Heart-rending was their anguish when they were told that he was already a week buried. These and numberless cases of like character indicate what war is, even when viewed from a favourable standpoint

All the clothing of the wounded soldiers was carried at once to our new steam laundry, where it underwent a most thorough washing and disinfection. This clothing was, for the most part, stiff with mud, saturated with blood and badly torn. When dried it was given back to those in charge of the army. The Sisters and servant-maids performed this work. They were assisted by the women refugees of Willebroeck, whose houses were burned off on account of the fortress. Washing took place every day and continued until late in the night.

The condition of the poor maimed soldiers was sad to behold. One man, we were told by the Red Cross nurses, had twenty bullets in his body; another was pierced through the lung by a bayonet; one, aged hand; one was crazed by a bullet which touched the brain; another was shot through the mouthy the bullet lodging in the back of the throat. His case was especially distressing, his the most intense suffering of all. He lived for a week without eating, drinking or speaking.

Three wounded Germans were brought in, being picked up on the battle field by members of our division of the Red Cross. They seemed greatly distressed and afraid, positively refusing to touch food or drink of which the Sisters or nurses did not first partake. One was a German lieutenant, under whose direction, as he himself admitted, great damage had been done in one of the large cities. He was given the distinction of a bed among the Belgian officers. He was very ill at ease in their presence, in the beginning, but becoming reassured and observing the impartiality of sisters and nurses, he desired to remain in our hospital rather than be removed to a third post.

One day we were called upon to witness a most sorrowful sight. A small farmer's wagon drove up to the gate, bearing the lifeless bodies of two children, a girl aged eight and her brother, aged fourteen. The mother and a smaller child were also in the wagon. The mother related that they were taking flight as refugees. Seeing the enemy, they hastened to retreat, and were fired at by the soldiers. The children, who were in the back part of the wagon, were struck and wounded in a most frightful manner. The little girl's face was nearly all torn off, and the back of the boy's head had been shattered.

At the approach of Belgian soldiers, who fired at the enemy, the mother was enabled to pick up the lifeless bodies of her children, put them into the wagon and drive with them to our hospital, which was the nearest post.

These people were from Nieuwenrode, Province of Brabant. It was said that many German soldiers were in ambush, in this region, although no battle had occurred there. The Doctors Van Everbroeck and DeLatte, who examined the bodies of these children, stated that they were shot at a distance of twenty meters.

The mother, suffering greatly from the shock, and the remaining child were taken to the village hospital.

Flour, soap and washing soda were supplied by the government for the use of the soldiers. The sisters performed the work and used a great deal of their own provisions for the wounded. A large quantity of linen for sheets, gowns and hand towels, was supplied by the "*Chef*" of the Red Cross. The sisters, when not engaged in other work, spent the time in folding, hemming and stitching these articles and in preparing surgical dressings for the wounded.

Several sisters and at least two lady nurses remained in charge of the different wards day and night. The most perfect order and discipline prevailed. The wounded soldiers who were at all able to get around walked in the garden or rested and visited with their families, who came to see them.

The tender care of mothers for their children could not surpass the devoted kindness of the members of the Red Cross in their services to the wounded. Nothing that could be done to assist or alleviate their sufferings was omitted. The soldiers were to each other as brothers of one family. We have seen them carrying in, on stretchers, their weary, foot-sore comrades, and with the tenderest care take of! the clumsy, muddy shoes, gently strip the blistered feet of the coarse stockings and, on bended knees, bathe and bandage them.

The first division of the Red Cross which came to our Hospital was with us about five weeks. One evening about seven o'clock, some time after Brussels had been occupied by the Germans, a dispatch came to the "*chef*" commanding the Red Cross to leave Willebroeck at once and go to another station. Again there was hurrying to and fro.

155

The large wagon was opened and everything hastily packed in. In the different wards the poor wounded soldiers, obliged to leave their beds, were sitting silent and motionless, while tears were in their eyes. Later in the night motor cars came and took them all away. The German lieutenant, on account of the condition in which he was found by the physicians, could not be removed at that time and remained until the departure of the second ambulance.

Preparations for the departure of the Red Cross continued most of the night. With the continual running back and forth, and the noise produced by taking up and laying down boxes and bundles, there was no rest to be obtained.

Before seven in the morning all the wards were empty. One or two soldiers, whose condition did not permit of their removal, still remained. All noise and commotion had ceased and the silence of death reigned in the house.

A day or two of repose would have been a welcome boon to the sisters, who were much fatigued at that time. However, rest was impossible, as we obtained a message that another division of the Red Cross was on its way to our hospital. So it happened that all the rooms and various apartments had to be cleaned and rearranged at once. This work took place immediately. Two days later, although the pungent smell of disinfectants still pervaded the air, every ward was as neat and clean as if no wounded soldiers, no death, nor sorrow had entered there.

We did not know the cause of the sudden departure of the Red Cross, as the strictest secrecy was observed by the officers of the army; but we remarked a little later that this departure was necessary on account of the rapid advance of the fast-approaching enemy and the evident possibility of a heavy pitched battle at the fortress. In such a case the convalescent could not remain longer than was absolutely necessary. They were obliged to go in order to make place for the numerous wounded who were yet to come.

CHAPTER 9

The Return of the Army

A little after four o'clock one afternoon, shortly before the departure of the first division of the Red Cross, our attention was attracted by the heavy and continuous tread of cavalry and soldiers passing along the street. It was the Belgian Army returning from a long and tiresome march.

Here was found a different kind of suffering from that which was ministered to in the hospital. Hunger and fatigue were stamped upon the countenance of each of these men, who, about a month before were industrious citizens at their daily occupations.

We saw them marching away in the early morning some time before, full of courage and patriotic zeal. For what reason they all marched off, or where they were going, we knew not; but were informed later by one of the officers that while on the march they had been attacked by the enemy, who were stealthily concealed, and fired into their ranks from both sides of the road. Several of the soldiers were killed and a large number wounded, but, having retreated promptly and in order, no great loss of life was sustained.

There were in the ranks priests, in their long black cassocks, wearing the arm-band of the Red Cross, who, as volunteer chaplains, had joined the army and were ever at the service of the soldiers on the march, and even on the battle field. We were informed that priests, and those preparing for the priesthood, were not obliged to serve in the army in times of peace; but, in case of war, they may be called upon to serve as military chaplains. When the present war broke out, hundreds of them joined as volunteers, marching in the ranks with the soldiers and undergoing their sufferings and hardships.

Many doctors rode along in motor cars. They were distinguished by a special dark-coloured uniform, with a red collar and gilded trimmings. They also wore the armband of the Red Cross. Officers on horseback led each division of the army. The faces of all were disfigured with sweat and dust, while dust in abundance covered shoes and clothing. Some were staggering along, unable to walk straight, owing to the hard shoes and blistered feet. Hollow-cheeked, and with eyes which seemed to protrude from their sockets, they passed along, piteously imploring a morsel of bread.

Fortunately, the abundant supply of bread in the convent had just been increased by the addition of forty of those immense loaves found only in Belgium. All of this was hastily cut, buttered and, with baskets full of pears, dealt out, piece by piece, to the passing soldiers, until, finally, only a small portion remained over for the supper of the wounded remaining in the hospital.

The servant maids went out to the village later in search of bread, but there was not a loaf to be found anywhere. All had been given to the soldiers. Two sisters and one of the maids remained up all night. The oven was again heated and the usual supply of bread doubled.

Every large *locale* in the village from which, by the way, all non-resident refugees were obliged to depart, received the various divisions of the army which were allotted to them. About two hundred soldiers were assigned to those parts of our Parochial School unoccupied by the village refugees or not in use by the Red Cross.

Before the command was given to enter the schools, we saw soldiers, among whom were also priests, lying on the ground on the opposite side of the street, even as horses which, having run a great distance, fall down from sheer exhaustion. Some of these, we learned afterwards, did not have their shoes off in nearly three weeks. The socks, hard and worn out, were in some cases stamped into the blistered feet in such a manner as to cause excruciating pain. In some cases the feet were so painful and swollen that the patients had to be carried in on stretchers. In the meantime, several ambulance wagons had stopped at the school gate, and numerous wounded were carried in.

When finally one division entered *d'Externat*, a hasty search was begun for hay and straw. All that could be found was carried into the garret of the schools and the empty classrooms.

The refugees of Willebroeck were very generous to the soldiers, giving them all the provisions which they could find. Many soldiers were seen with pails in their hands in search of water. Of this there was a good supply on the place, and more could readily be obtained at the cistern which was connected with the canal. In a short time they were refreshed and cleansed from the dust and sweat of that long and tiresome march, and were observed sitting in groups on the grass which surrounded the school.

Soon after a large door, which one of the refugees carried away from his house in the village before it was burned, was found. This was laid on two small heaps of stone, so as to form a table. About half an ox was procured and a large part of it chopped into small pieces and put into a big iron kettle, which was then filled with water. The kettle was placed on a wood fire kindled in the garden, and potatoes and other ingredients put into it. After a time it began to boil in a lively manner, greatly to the satisfaction of those poor hungry men who were so patiently waiting for their supper. When this finally was ready, the knapsacks were opened and each took out a spoon and a small tin can, the cover of which served for plate, cup and saucer.

Probably the German General Staff failed to enjoy their bounteous supper that evening as well as did the poor Belgian soldiers their soup on the cool green grass. It must be remarked that each division was under the direction of an officer, who placed armed guards at the gates and passages. Perfect order prevailed. They talked quietly among themselves and remained strictly within the places assigned to their use; only once in a while one of them would knock at the kitchen door and ask for a can of water, which was soon understood to mean a can of cold coffee. This was never refused, and the grateful "*Mercie*" (thanks) was ample reward for the service rendered.

That night passed quietly. The soldiers had a good opportunity to rest on the hay and straw which had been provided. Some of them were astir at a very early hour. The large kettle was again placed over the fire and filled with water for the soldiers' breakfast of bread and black coffee. Their only fear was that a message to depart would arrive before they would have a chance of "*Coffie drinken*" (drinking coffee, or breakfast).

At about eight o'clock one evening during the stay of the soldiers an excited group of eight men and two boys ran wildly into the yard through the gate, which had been left open for the soldiers not yet arrived. Great drops of sweat were on their faces. They were out of breath from running, and greatly excited. Some were bare-footed, having lost or thrown away their wooden shoes in the great haste to escape the enemy, who, they related, had entered a village three or four miles distant and had taken as prisoners a number of citizens and placed them in front of their own ranks. The boys had lost their parents in the confusion which ensued and were crying bitterly. They found a resting place somewhere in the schools that night and departed early next morning, because non-resident refugees were not permitted to remain after the arrival of the Red Cross.

The soldiers were called away several times for short intervals, after which they again returned for a rest. Thus the month of August passed. The frightful campaign progressed slowly but surely. Several times we had seen the hostile aeroplane, with its shining armour glittering in the sunshine, flying gracefully over our schools. How we then feared for our wounded, so helplessly lying within these same walls. One morning, about three o'clock, we were suddenly awakened by heavy, oft-repeated shooting, which seemed to proceed from the farther end of our garden. The alarm was caused by the appearance of an aeroplane soaring as a huge bird over the fortress. *Mettrailleusen* opened fire upon it, and the unwelcome visitor soon disappeared. However, we all feared its reappearance in the night. For this reason the towns and cities were kept in total darkness from eight o'clock in the evening, and searchlights illumined the dark clouds over and around the fortresses and other places of particular importance.

About this time we were informed that several thousand of the enemy's soldiers were digging trenches and fortifying themselves on all sides of us. Every newspaper brought fresh tidings of most inhuman atrocities which filled the minds of the people with unspeakable horror.

In Belgium it was neither the German nation nor her soldiers, considered as a whole, who were held responsible for these awful outrages, because it was well known that there were among them many noble characters and Christians, renowned for their piety and fidelity to God and country, who were sacrificing their lives for what they thought to be a just and holy cause and whose families were also suffering and sorrowing at home.

It was alone, as should be known by everyone, the Godless element in the German Army, led on and sustained by equally Godless officers, who encouraged, permitted and probably commanded those crimes, as we infer from the testimony of German wounded soldiers in our Red Cross hospitals. "If we do not shoot, burn and pillage," said one of them, "we shall be shot ourselves."

It seems incredible that anyone claiming Christian convictions of any creed or country, could have acted as did the so-called barbarians who despoiled many of the most beautiful cities, towns and villages of Belgium.

CHAPTER 10

Anxious Days

Early one morning, while passing through the yard, we heard what seemed to be peals of distant thunder. We looked around to see if a storm was approaching, but as the sun shone brightly and not a cloud was to be seen in the sky, we soon realized what this dismal sound implied. On entering the convent, we found several of our members standing by the map of Belgium, tracing the route of portions of the German Army then endeavouring to force their way through to Antwerp.

The firing heard in the garden came from the bombardment of the City of Mechelen. The first attack did not continue so long, nor was the damage so great, as in the attacks which followed. The noise of the cannonade increased from that day forward. Hardly a day or night passed without bringing the unwelcome sound from one or the other direction. It often happened that, having retired at a late hour after a long and fatiguing day's work, the short repose was interrupted by the explosion of bombs or cannon bails, which, although then at a safe distance from our village, was none the less terrifying.

In this most cruel war battles continued in the night as well as in the day. When time was asked by either army to remove the wounded, it was refused, because each mistrusted the motives of the other, thinking that, instead of removing the wounded, they would utilize the time thus gained in preparing for another attack.

About the first of September we went to Antwerp for a day or two. While on the train we saw the wires stretched from place to place, and heard explained the intended use of electricity at the fortress. Antwerp was at that time, still and peaceful, as a child who slumbered, feeling perfectly safe within her lines of fortifications. About eight o'clock in the evening every light had to be put out, and the place resembled a city of the dead.

On returning about twelve o'clock on Sunday, with the Sister who accompanied me, we found some wounded brought in, who were pierced by bayonets at a short distance from our house. Their condition was critical, but they recovered sufficiently to be taken to Antwerp within the following week.

A day or two later, while crossing the yard, we suddenly heard that sissing, crackling sound of a shell or bomb flying through the air in the direction of the church spire which towered above the walls of the convent chapel. Several others followed in quick succession. All the convalescent soldiers who were in the yard, the Sisters and ladies in the garden, hastened to take refuge in the cellars.

We feared for the wounded soldiers within, who could not leave their beds. Soon the attack was answered by a heavy volley from the fortress, and the cannonade continued until early next morning.

A day or two later one of the refugees visited the place where the cannonade of the fortress had swept the entire region as if a tornado had passed over it. On returning he related that parts of human bodies hung on the trees and filled the hedges.

When the danger became imminent, the older sisters and those who were ill, or in any way disabled, were advised by the Rev. Superior to seek refuge in the more secluded mission houses of the community, and to. all who desired, permission was given to do the same, or to return to their families for the time being. This was done on account of the inadvisability of anyone's remaining at the convent during a battle, since the buildings were in close proximity to the fortress.

Some of the sisters packed their trunks and sent them to the homes of their families. This precaution did not avail much, as the families of many of our members had to leave their homes as refugees and probably lost all their personal property.

Although all were permitted to seek safety in other places, only the older members and two or three of the younger sisters availed themselves of the opportunity. All save these gathered around the Superior and her assistant, and promised voluntarily to remain to the very last to assist in the care of the wounded, whose number increased daily since the arrival of the second division of the Red Cross.

On several occasions spies were arrested in Willebroeck and taken away. Some were arrested in Brussels and Antwerp in the garb of priests. It was authoritatively reported that supplies of weapons and ammunition, among which was dynamite, were found in public buildings in Antwerp, carefully hidden away in the basements. This aroused distrust on the part of the Belgians for the resident Germans, whom they had always treated with the greatest confidence and respect.

The result was that all the Germans then in Belgium were expelled from the country and had to return to their own land. This was, indeed, a hardship for the unoffending resident Germans, whose homes for years had been in the cities and towns of this little kingdom.

We retired at a late hour one night amid the incessant booming of cannon. Scarcely were our eyes closed when someone passed in the dormitory and knocked at each door. "*Ave Maria*" was the quiet greeting. "*Deo Gratias*," the response. "What is it?" was asked. "The Germans have entered and are crossing the bridge," was the reply.

With beating heart and trembling limbs, each sprang up and was dressed in a few minutes. In a state of great excitement, all stood in the hall ready to receive orders from the Superior, who had gone downstairs to make inquiries about the situation. At the first sound of the alarm a party of soldiers and their officer went out to ascertain the facts in the case, as the bridge where the enemy were said to be crossing was not far distant.

All the inhabitants of the village were on the alert. By the time the sisters were ready to depart, the soldiers had returned, whose officer laughingly related that it was only a party of Belgian "*Landers*" in gray uniform, whom the *burgomaster* of Blaesvelt had mistaken for German soldiers, and thought it his duty to spread the alarm.

All retired quietly to their rooms once more, but no one rested much the remainder of the night.

Then followed anxious days for the residents of Willebroeck, who expected momentarily to hear the alarm clock in the church tower give notice to flee for their lives. The officers of the Belgian Army were very sanguine, and assured the Superior and those in charge of the wounded that timely notice would be given if the danger increased.

Nevertheless, the crackling of shells, the heavy cannonade from the fortress and field cannon, and the occasional proximity of those hostile aeroplanes, together with the reports of atrocities and destruction taking place around us, were fearsome in the extreme.

In striking contrast to the noise and commotion on all sides, was the calm tranquillity which reigned in the chapel. The Sacred Heart stretched forth that same Fatherly hand which assisted the apostle sinking on the Sea of Galilee. The altar was still and solitary, but the little red light flickered in the sanctuary lamp and told of Him whose word alone stilled the winds and calmed the angry waves.

In the circumstances which then existed, one would almost envy the dead resting so quietly in the old-time vault, in the shadow of the tabernacle.

Lights were forbidden after a certain hour, but the moon shone through the stained windows and wrought fantastic designs on the gilded moulding, while the mild and peaceful looks which character-ise the images of the saints told of heroism and victories won on the battlefield of life, in the pursuit of peace and sanctity, and carried the mind to that future and better life where neither the pride, avarice, nor ambition of man can ever destroy the eternal peace, nor break the impregnable union of hearts.

The Flight of the Refugees

While the aforesaid events were taking place, sorrowful scenes were witnessed along the streets. Our attention and sympathies were particularly attracted to the flight of the refugees. In this case we could give no material assistance, as we were able to do in other cases.

For hours and days and weeks the doleful procession passed along the streets; a living stream made up of all ranks and classes of society. Here were seen the poor old farmer's household, whose sons had gone to the front; and young married women, with small children in their arms or by their sides, whose husbands had to don the soldier's uniform and go to the war. The sick, the old and the feeble were taken from their beds of suffering and, with shawls or blankets thrown over their shoulders, placed in carts or wagons and carried away, perhaps, to perish by the roadside. We have seen cripples and small children hurriedly driven along the street in wheelbarrows.

Packages carried on their arms, on their backs, or in little carts were about all that the poor people could take, and all that they desired, so confident were they of a speedy return to their homes.

On another day about the end of August, the unbroken line which filed through the street at noon was, without any interruption, passing through at twelve o'clock that night. As the cities, towns and villages were, for the most part, taken by surprise, or bombarded without having received any notice, the civilians had no alternative but to collect a few necessary articles of clothing, and in some cases a loaf of bread, and flee in haste from their homes, leaving crops, cattle, furniture and all their possessions to the fury of the flames and the tide of destruction, so rapidly sweeping down upon them.

Many people of the wealthier class, anticipating what was to come, had packed trunks and boxes with clothing and other personal prop-

165

erty and sent them away to what was considered safe quarters. Then they moved away within the fortifications of Antwerp, where it was thought the enemy could not enter. Others, in the firm hope that the war would soon be over and that they would be able to return to their homesteads in a few days, left everything untouched and fled from city to village and from town to town. We met parties of acquaintances in Antwerp who had changed their places of residence nine times within one month, and then were obliged to leave Antwerp in a day or two.

Some let their cattle run loose in the meadows. These were shot down or taken by the soldiers, or appropriated by any one who desired.

It was most pitiful to see these poor people, whose only object was to get away as far as possible from the scenes of conflict. Some carried small loaves of bread; others had a little hay or straw in their wagons; some led a cow or two; others two or three pigs. In some of the carts we recognised faces of our former pupils, who only one short month before were longing for the pleasant vacation days. Their fathers or brothers were in the army, and their homes forsaken. Some children had lost their parents and were crying piteously. When the Sisters left the parish church, where they daily took part in the public devotions for peace, they were besieged by hundreds of these poor, half-frantic refugees, beseeching shelter over night in the church or schools, which were already full to overflowing. The days were warm and pleasant, but the nights were very chilly and sometimes rainy. Where would those poor people go and what could they do without food or shelter for all those little children? The friendly stars looked down from the realms above upon thousands who lay along the roadside, while others crowded the barns and country schools, or made rude tent-like shelters in the bed of the new canal.

This canal would have been opened in September with great festivities, over which King Albert was expected to preside.

Peace or security was nowhere to be found. The war-chased people fled from place to place for weeks, fearful and famishing, until the kindly and protecting arms of England and Holland received them, and the noble hearts and hands of American women united to provide food and clothing for those who fled, and for the others also who would not, or could not, leave their own country.

While cheerfully and gratefully testifying to what has been accomplished in this country, and the great amount of money spent in alleviating the sufferings caused by this sanguinary conflict, it does seem sad to think that American manufacturers will continue to supply weapons and ammunition to any of the belligerent countries. It reminds one of a great conflagration, in which the firemen exert themselves to subdue the flames, while a few pour on oil to replenish the fire. This will be a lasting reproach to those engaged in this destroying traffic. *"There is no pocket in a shroud,"* and the bloodstained money obtained in this manner will not assuage the pain and grief of the orphan and widow, nor will it purchase redemption at the judgment seat above.

As the danger increased, difficulties in the way of travelling also increased. Passports, upon which were indicated the distinguishing characteristics of the bearer, had to be obtained before leaving one's place of residence, if only for one hour; and such passports could only be used in the vicinity in which they were issued.

To go to Antwerp, or any of the cities or towns at a distance, one's passport had to bear his or her portrait, sealed by the *burgomaster* of the town or city wherein he resided. If these requirements were not complied with, a person would not be permitted to pass through the gate of a city or enter even an ordinary depot.

A great number of refugees found their way ultimately within the fortified city of Antwerp. They were seen for a day or two in solitary groups in the public park, or in tents along the streets. In a large school near the Palace of Justice fifteen hundred found refuge for a few days, and were then directed to leave.

The authorities, becoming alarmed about the food and water supplies of the city, and fearing contagion or disease, compelled all refugees who were not obliged to leave their homes on account of fortifications, to leave the city within a specified time. Large numbers of these poor, homeless people, many of whom were of gentle birth and wealthy, were obliged to crowd into freight cars which had been used for the transportation of cattle, and were thus carried away to Ghent or Ostend. From Ostend they were shipped to England. Many had previously left Antwerp for Holland. In these countries thousands of them will prayerfully await the dawn of peace, which will decide the future destiny of their country.

The events already related occurred between the first of August and the 27th of September. Sunday, September 27, passed off quietly in Willebroeck, although refugees filed through the streets continually, and the booming of cannon was heard in the surrounding towns. The sky was leaden and a sombre, smoky atmosphere hung over the country and caused a feeling of sadness and uncertainty.

In the evening one of the refugees returned from a hurried visit to the scene of his former home, and related to his daughter, who anxiously awaited his arrival, that the enemy had made great headway, "Tomorrow will be the last day in which it will be safe to remain in Willebroeck," said he to those who stood there.

In a few minutes the report was circulated on all sides. Sisters, on hearing it, remarked, "Nonsense! What God protects is well protected; we must not be alarmed, but patiently await the accomplishment of God's holy will." Monday's papers brought news of another bombardment of the City of Mechelen (Malines), a short distance from Willebroeck.

Following are a few quotations from that morning's paper (Antwerp's *Handelsblad*, Monday, September 28, 1914):

While on the train this morning, before entering the station of Mechelen, our attention was attracted by the multitudes who, in the greatest haste, took flight through the Zandpoortvest They were the residents of Muysen, The German troops, about eight hundred strong, were there at half-past seven; thus the people had no alternative but to take flight as rapidly as possible. The enemy shot upon some refugees, and the ten-year-old son of Desiré Horckmans was shot in the car where he was sitting, and Mrs. Arm Beulens was seriously wounded.

This was only a sign of what was yet to come.

Scarcely had we reached the station, at half-past eight, when we heard the heavy roar of cannon, followed by terrific explosions, such as we had never before heard. All the people who had come from the direction of Antwerp took flight through the side streets. At every explosion it seemed as if an earthquake shook the ground under foot. So heavy were the shocks that many people fell.

On the Schuttersvest, we found refuge in a cellar, while one volley followed another. The explosions were deafening. Every pane of glass in the vicinity was broken in pieces. In several places the stones were forced out of the pavements and thrown to a great distance, while bombs pierced the ground to the depth of two meters.

One can judge the terror in which the residents of Mechelen tried to find a place of safety. The cannonade was awful, as was also the '*gesis*' (sissing noise) of the bombs which flew over the streets and, exploding, spread fire, death and destruction in every direction.

A bomb fell just in front of the railroad station, making a pit in the ground three 'metres' in diameter. The place was covered with stones, which were violently jerked out of the ground. The station is half-demolished. No one is there to be seen except the lifeless body of an elderly gentleman who, with his face to the ground, is stretched out on the floor of the waiting-room.

The beautiful buildings belonging to the Little Sisters of the Poor, and many other noted buildings have been totally destroyed. Thus it was in the few places which we have visited. What will it be in other places? All the streets through which we passed were covered with glass and stones. In all the city there is not a pane of glass which remains whole. All day long the Duffel highway was black with refugees, which makes us conclude that all Mechelen has taken flight.

CHAPTER 12

The Results of War

Centuries ago, when Attila, known in history as the "Scourge of God," led his army of Huns through the fertile fields of Europe, we read that he gazed upon the ruin which he had caused his soldiers to perpetrate on all sides, and cried out, "*I am the hammer of the world, the grass grows no more where my horse has trod.*"

Well may these same words be applied to the armed forces now dominating the devastated plains and meadows of what was once peaceful Belgium.

When one passes through the masses of falling debris and looks upon the remains of cities and villages which have stood for ages and in whose monuments and public buildings a more than human strength and beauty seemed enclosed, it appears that the Angel of Destruction has extended his deadly sceptre over the works of man and congealed those streams of life which once flowed through the streets now deserted and homes made desolate by the unheard-of ferocity of civilised man.

When we try to estimate the amount of time, labour, wealth and industry required to build up these beautiful places, now stripped of their grandeur, devoid of life, and crumbling into dust, we become awestruck at sight of such desolation. The nothingness of the much-prized materialism becomes apparent in the ruins of man's grandest achievements, and involuntarily we are moved to cry out, "Vanity of vanities! all is vanity," which the evolutions of time can change into dust and ashes.

Again the cruel hand of war is seen in the country homes, whose rustic beauty among the groves and green meadows so often aroused the spirit of song and fascinated the lover of Nature in his rambles. The churches whose cross-crowned spires, wherein the "*klokken*"

170

(chimes) so often pealed forth the call to prayer, are now abandoned, and their battered walls and broken windows look sadly down upon the deserted homesteads from which life has passed away.

The schools no more re-echo the gay sounds of children's voices, while the famishing little ones and their destitute parents are dying of hunger and privation or begging at the stranger's door. The colleges and libraries have delivered their volumes to the fury of the flames, and the withering blight has scorched the fresh verdure of those well-kept gardens and shady lawns where kings and princes dwelt.

Castles have been made into fortresses to conceal cannon and machine guns, while the deafening roar of exploding bombs replaces the gay music of ball and banquet room.

The red glow of the burning city illumines the evening sky and reveals in the darkness the ghastly spectres of partially demolished walls of the stateliest buildings which stand out amid the ever-increasing ruins.

War has desecrated the churches where angels knelt around the Holy of Holies, and where the daily Holocaust of Love, and the offering of praise and prayers perpetuated communion between earth and heaven. Have the angels left the altar at sight of the sacrilege committed in their presence, or did they weep when the merciless bomb struck die house of God and wounded the worshipers there?

Behold the terror-stricken congregation leaving St. Rombout's Cathedral and taking flight through the streets of Mechelen, amid the falling walls and bursting pavements. Weeks later we shall meet them again as refugees in London, Leeds and Bradford, seeking food and shelter in the land of exile.

See that little coffin, less than two feet long! It seems so conspicuous, exposed there among the coffins of several soldiers who died that night in our hospital. This small casket contained the remains of a little angel about two months old, who was struck in the arms of her mother by a piece of exploded shell.

This woman had hurriedly left her home during the second bombardment of the city of Mechelen and, having run for some distance, sat down by the way to rest, when the fatal shell exploded, a piece of which mortally wounded the little one in her arms. Both were brought to our hospital that night and lovingly cared for until about morning, when the innocent spirit fled to join the army of the blessed who inherit the realms of eternal peace.

Poor mother was left alone to bemoan the loss of her little one and to weep over her desolate home.

When one meets the ambulance wagons loaded with suffering, mutilated men who a few weeks before were sustaining heads of happy households; when one sees the dark red stream flowing from ghastly wounds and splashes of blood on all sides; when one observes the pallor of death on the strong man's face, while a comrade with tender pity bends over to obtain a last message for home; when one hears the despairing wail of orphan and widow; when one has watched the endless procession of terror-stricken refugees whose homes have become the prey of the cannon, when one hears repeatedly the sad experience of these exiles on their journeys from place to place, lying on hay or straw, in barns, in schools, on the bare ground, or in the basin of the empty canal, when one meditates on those perverse circumstances which have changed civilised men into savage brutes—then we also agree that "*The world has gone back a thousand years*," while a presentiment as of impending disaster passes over the earth and depresses each individual heart.

"Cast yourselves upon the knees and pray for victory," cry out Christian monarchs to their soldiers, and, nevertheless, the God to whom they pray is witness to the wanton desecration of His churches and the wholesale destruction of life, liberty and property.

From the dark abodes of despair, the *cohorts* of Satan seem to have taken possession of the world and filled it with vice and wretchedness, until it resembles the "abomination of desolation" referred to in Holy Writ.

To know what war is, it would be necessary to possess eyes to behold all the sin and vice; all the ruin and destruction; ears to hear every despairing cry and agonising wail; a mind to comprehend all the misery and desolation, and a heart to feel the anguish in the heart of each suffering fellow-creature, from the moment the first shot was fired down through ages yet to come, until the twilight of times, brighter in prospect, than the daylight of the present generation shall obscure the last shadows of the unholy conflict.

To realise what war really means, we should give consideration to the moral and physical degeneration of these sufferers and of their descendants; to the hatred, lust, passion, wilful murder and other high crimes against God and nature, engendered and committed, not in the moment of strong individual anger and passion, but as the result of a well-calculated plan, with profound forethought, called by some "strategy."

"War is justifiable only, if it is the necessary means for securing peace." (His Eminence, Cardinal Mercier.) May we humbly add, *then only as the last resort.*

CHAPTER 13

Our Departure

Monday, September 28, witnessed the scenes of sorrow and desolation in and around Mechelen and vicinity described in the foregoing chapters. Many of the residents of Willebroeck had already taken flight, and the others were preparing to leave.

The sisters, wholly absorbed in their work for the wounded, and relying on the word of the Belgian officers, that timely warning would be given as to the necessity of departure, had as yet no idea of joining the throngs of refugees who continuously filed through the main street.

The shocks of the cannonade from the fortress caused the buildings to tremble on their foundations, while the ground under foot seemed agitated as by an earthquake. A large number of wounded soldiers had been brought in the night before, and three or four lay dead in the mortuary.

Our sisters and servant maids, as also the generous women refugees of Willebroeck, continued their sickening task in the laundry. In wooden shoes they stood at those large cement tubs while suds and blood-dyed water streamed over the stone floor.

Since the cutting of the electric wires the motor which kept the machines in action could no longer be used for the laundry or for the bakery. This greatly increased the work in both places.

Large, vicious-looking black flies, before unseen in or about the place, probably attracted by the odour of blood, buzzed around in a most disagreeable manner.

The whole scene left an ineffaceable impression of sadness and horror at the unwonted ferocity of civilized man.

Night closed in again, but brought neither rest nor consolation. Fearing to retire, some of the sisters remained in the chapel, while others spent the tedious hours of that dreary night in the refectory or adjoining rooms, and kept busy making surgical dressings for the wounded, of whom a larger number than usual had been brought into the hospital.

At intervals during the night the cannonade was heard, while the searchlights of the fortress penetrated the clouds on the lookout for the murderous Zeppelins. Morning came at last, with an increase of work and anguish. The enemy, with their usual determination, were trying to force their way through to Antwerp, while the Belgians were equally determined to prevent them, or to at least check their progress.

On Tuesday, September 29, the daily routine of the convent took place as usual until noon, when the cannonade became terrific. A balloon, the meaning of which we did not know, had been sent up by the enemy. Some said it was to discover the position of the Belgians and, if possible, ascertain their strength. The Reverend Superior called upon one of the officers and asked if there was danger. "No," said he, "We shall let you know in due time."

Three sisters, intending to go to Antwerp, sent a messenger to the station to ask when the train would leave. "No trains until evening," was the reply. They decided to wait until that time. Just then another officer called for the Reverend Superior and said in an excited manner, "*Weg van hier, aanstonds! Geen tijd te verliezen.*" (Away from here at once. No time to be lost.) This message flew from one to another, even to the terror-stricken hearts of the numerous wounded.

Impossible to describe the scenes which followed. In a few minutes a long line of motor cars came whirling up to the gate to take away the wounded who, some of them in an almost dying condition, were being dragged out of their beds, dressed and hurriedly carried away to Antwerp, or to another place of refuge. One can never forget the look of anguish on some of their faces, while others seemed totally indifferent to all that was taking place around them.

There was one who was not indifferent. It was the wounded German officer who, as he himself admitted, had accomplished so much in the destruction of Louvain, and whose serious condition did not permit his being transferred with the first division of the Red Cross which left a short time before. He was sorely troubled when he heard he had to leave, and would much rather have remained. He promised, in case the opportunity offered, to speak a good word for the convent.

175

Did he survive or obtain his freedom, and thus have occasion to keep his word? We know not; but we do know that when the German soldiers were in possession of our Boarding-school, after the fall of Antwerp, our Superior and sisters wrote that they had no complaint to make as to the conduct of those *"Rynlanders."*

The sisters could hardly realise that they were obliged to leave their convent home, for which they had toiled and laboured for years, and which was as dear to them as the arms of a mother to her children; those schools which had so often re-echoed to the gay sounds of children's voices, as hundreds of them marched and sang in chorus; the garden where the white ducks were yet swimming in the pond; the fruit trees and flowers; in a word, all had to be left to the fire of the merciless bombs and shrapnels.

Several times they went back and forth, while it seemed preferable to remain and take the risk than to go and endure the vicissitudes of pilgrimage and exile. But the command had to be obeyed, as the danger increased every moment.

About two o'clock three of us joined the crowds of farmers, country people and cavalrymen who were passing on their way to Boom. The other sisters stood in the hall, ready to depart. We carried satchels and some small baggage, and walked to Boom, where we arrived safely at three o'clock. On the way we met a lady and gentleman who conversed fluently in English.

When we arrived at the station we learned that the train for Antwerp had left a few minutes before, and there would be no further transportation before evening. We went to the home of one of our sisters in Boom and rested until five o'clock. Here we were joined by our Rev. Mother Superior and a large party of sisters, who had left Willebroeck shortly after we did. Just as they had crossed the bridge of Boom, a bomb fell beside it and exploded, but did not injure the bridge. Our sisters were on their way to Aertselaar, one of our missions at some distance from the firing line. Rev. Father Somers, one of the assistant priests of Willebroeck, remained at his post in the village church during the bombardment of the town. Four sisters had the courage to remain in the convent when all the rest had left. They have written recently from Bristol, England, describing their experience amid the rain of bombs and shrapnel which fell that evening in the garden and around the buildings.

Bidding *adieu* to the sisters who had joined us in Boom, we went to the railroad station about five o'clock in the evening, expecting to be in good time for the train to Antwerp. One of the sisters sent a dispatch to her mother to send some one to meet us in the East Station when the train would arrive. As we approached the station in Boom, we met throngs of people coming back.

A lady told us not to go to the station, as no train would leave for Antwerp that night. Undismayed by the sad news, we passed those crowds of people and went right on to the station. The station-master was not at liberty, so we stood there a few moments with a party of others in the waiting-room. A young lady of Boom, one of our former pupils, and one of the sisters set out in search of a motor car or carriage. None could be obtained at any cost, not even a farmer's cart or wagon. All that could be used were in the service of the army.

From five o'clock until seven, the fruitless search continued, while the other two sisters remained at the station in charge of the baggage. At seven o'clock one sister returned with the good news that she had met the "*chef*" of the First Division of the Red Cross ambulance which had remained in our hospital, and, having exhausted all the fine expressions in her French vocabulary, at last succeeded in sending him to the general of the Belgian Army, then in a restaurant in the city, to ask permission for the sisters to enter the train of the Red Cross, which was at that time standing on the Antwerp Railroad, back of the depot.

A lady and gentleman of Antwerp, on hearing of our success, pleaded with tears in their eyes to have us ask permission for them also to enter the train. Our youngest Sister, moved with compassion at the sorry plight of two fellow-creatures, made use of a stratagem in their favour. "Papa, Mamma," said she, when the "*chef*" approached with permission for the sisters to enter the train, "Papa, Mamma, carry our baggage into the train." The lady and gentleman took up the baggage in a hurry and the sisters followed them into the train.

It was just seven o'clock when we entered the train of the Red Cross, which then stood waiting for the wounded soldiers. Unfortunately for us, the wounded had been taken to Antwerp in motor cars and our train remained standing at the depot.

The heavy cannonade had somewhat abated, but the field cannon were yet heard in several directions, and we feared a return of the Zeppelins which had been flying over Antwerp the week before. We were doomed to disappointment as to our departure from Boom. It was too late and decidedly dangerous to return to the home of our Sisters in the city, and a long night in this stationary train seemed unendurable.

At twenty minutes to twelve the "*chef*" made his appearance once more and said that he had finally obtained permission to take the train to Antwerp; but we would be obliged to ride in the dark, very slowly, and arrive in a station at some distance from the usual stopping place. This depot was, nevertheless, known to the Sisters, who, if only safely in the city, felt sure of finding their way home. So the lights were turned out and the train started off. It was so dark that we could hardly distinguish the trees or buildings along the route.

CHAPTER 14

Arrival in Antwerp

Shortly after leaving Boom, the sounds of war died out entirely, and one felt that there was at least one haven of safety in Belgium. About half-past one in the night we entered the Bassins, a station near the docks of Antwerp. We thanked the good "*chef*" heartily and paid the station-master to accompany the party of five with a lantern to our destination. He did so, and on we walked the whole length of the *boulevard* to the Palace of Justice.

Antwerp, the chief port of Belgium, the centre of the railroad and canal systems, lay enshrouded in a cloak of darkness. Not the faintest glimmer of light was to be seen in the sky or on the land. Aside from this, there was not the slightest appearance of war, or of any disturbance whatever in the city.

At half-past two on Wednesday morning, September 30, hungry and utterly exhausted after the experience of the foregoing week, we rang at the residence of Madame Broelinckx, mother of one of the sisters of our company. This lady and her daughters received us with the greatest hospitality. They provided food and sleeping apartments, and left nothing undone to make our visit as pleasant and agreeable as could be under the circumstances. About three o'clock we retired for a few hours' rest, regardless of the dangerous Zeppelins which could have been flying over our heads. Next day we visited some of the magnificent churches in the city. These were filled to overflowing with pious worshipers at every service.

In the Church of the Jesuits, which we attended, it was difficult to find a seat, so great were the throngs who attended the evening devotions. The front scats were reserved for the convalescent soldiers, who attended in large numbers. It was so sad to see them. Some limped along on crutches; some with their broken arms in slings; while others had their heads and hands bandaged. Every door that opened or closed caused a shock, as if the bombs and cannon balls had followed us from Willebroeck.

We had never heard more zeal in the sermons, more confidence in the prayers, or more fervour in the responses, in which the entire congregation joined. We shall never, never forget that week of prayer in Antwerp.

In such circumstances, when the courage is about to fail at the approach of an inevitable doom which no human power can resist, then will the most haughty and indifferent fall on their knees and pray.

A day or two after our arrival in Antwerp, in company with the Misses Broelinckx, we visited the scenes of the Zeppelin raid which had taken place a few weeks before. It was sad to witness the damage done to those massive stone buildings. In some of them there was not a particle of glass to be seen in any of the window frames, while immense blocks of stone had been blown out of the walls. Bolts, knobs and bells were torn out of their places and the door demolished. One building looked as if it had been picked all over with a crowbar, while in some places pieces of the bomb had forced their way through the walls.

It was said in Antwerp that the bomb which fell back of the Bom street was aimed at the Palace of Justice, which is just at the corner of this street It was also stated that the aim taken by the enemy in throwing this bomb was only one millimetre from being perfect. If so, it deflected the difference of a whole block before it reached the ground.

Either nine or eleven bombs were said to have been thrown by Zeppelins in Antwerp long before the bombardment of that city. Not one, however, reached its destination, and only damaged the buildings and killed or wounded a few innocent residents.

On returning we met two sisters and a large number of orphan children, who left Willebroeck on the same day that we did. These Sisters, though similar to our own in some respects, had constant charge of the sick in the village hospital, which was founded and supported by the wealthy and charitable Lady of the Castle of Willebroeck, Madame De Naeyer. Besides a number of invalids, there were about one hundred orphan children in this institution when the bombardment of the village began.

One of the sisters said, that while carrying the invalids from their beds into the cellar, bombs were flying horizontally through the walls. One old woman was killed and another wounded. These two sisters then departed with the orphans and knew not what had become of the others.

At the urgent request of our kind hostess, and also in hope of receiving news from Willebroeck, or from the sisters with whom we had parted in Boom, we decided to remain over Sunday. The beginning of the following week passed uneventfully. One of our younger sisters joined us during the week, but had little to relate, not having heard from Willebroeck since our departure.

Greatly desiring to hear something from the convent, I resolved to ride over to Aertselaar with the milkmaid, as all the trains in this direction had ceased to run, and no other conveyance could be found. I went down to the park with Miss Broelinckx and waited until the good woman had sold all her milk, after which I climbed into the little wagon and we rode hastily in the direction of the city gates. When but a few yards from the large green "port" or gate, while waiting a few moments at a store, we were overtaken by Miss Broelinckx, who had hurried after us to announce that she had met the Reverend Superior and a large number of sisters, who had entered the city *en route* for Holland or England.

With unconcealed joy at the thought of meeting our sisters again, I bade *adieu* to the milkmaid and retraced my steps back to the house where our friends were assembled. After lunch, complications having arisen as to their departure for England, the sisters, about fifteen in number, decided to remain in the city for at least a few days. Some of them took up their residence with relatives, while the others found refuge in some of the convents in the city. It was arranged to hold a union meeting in a room adjoining the Jesuit Church, at which all were requested to be present, every day.

One of our party was quite despondent, owing to the fact that she had entirely lost track of her aged parents, who had left Mechelen during the bombardment of that city. A day or two later, while going to church, she had the pleasure of meeting her father on the street. He and his wife had come to Antwerp a few days before. They had found it necessary to change their place of residence nine times within one month. Mingled joy and sadness was felt a day or two later, when the Rev. Mother Superior visited the sisters at the home of Madame Broelinckx and described the condition of affairs at Willebroeck.

With the sisters whom we had left in Boom, she had gone to Aertselaar, where eight or ten of the older sisters were staying. This town, quite a distance from the city, was considered perfectly safe.

However, owing to the rapid approach of the enemy and the destruction of some of the fortresses, this place also became untenable. The city of Boom was evacuated and the bridge blown up a day or two after we left Willebroeck. Three days later all the refugees in Aertselaar were commanded to leave. This compelled the Reverend Superior to take the elder sisters, some of them hardly able to walk on account of age and debility, to the city of Antwerp. With great difficulty she had found a rude conveyance of some kind and rode on to the "port" of the city. When they reached the large gate it was discovered that the passports were not in perfect order, consequently the sisters were not allowed to enter.

Having found a resting-place for the others. Reverend Mother entered the city. After a short conference, she rode back to the sisters and we saw her no more. While with us she told of her narrow escape at the convent in Willebroeck the day after the sisters left.

On September 30, having left her charges in safety in Aertselaar, she rode back again to Willebroeck, where three sisters yet remained. The next day the cannonade was terrific.

CHAPTER 15

Extracts from Letters of Our Refugee Sisters

Following is an extract from a letter which came to hand on March 15, 1915, from the four sisters who remained in the convent throughout the bombardment, two of whom are now in charge of the Belgian refugees in Bristol, England:

As you already know, perhaps, three of us remained in our convent when all the rest had fled. Later in the afternoon we saw the Reverend Director and his sister step into the doctor's automobile and whirl off to a place of safety. Soon they were out of danger for the time being at least. That evening, following the advice of the Reverend Chaplain, we went to the Convent of the Presentation in Boom to pass the night. On the way we met Sister Michelle. When she heard that we had remained in Willebroeck, she came back with us. We were greatly pleased and took her along to Boom for the night. In the morning we returned to our Convent in Willebroeck in an automobile of the ambulance. There was work in abundance. We had to cook and bake for one hundred and twenty persons.

There were twenty priests with them. Besides these, there was scarcely any one left in Willebroeck. We rode to Antwerp for meat. Reverend Mother sent us word to come to Aertselaar to go with the other sisters to England. We went to Aertselaar and asked permission to remain in Willebroeck. Reverend Mother rode back with us. Again, in the afternoon, there was nothing to be heard but cannonade on all sides. Just as the Reverend Superior was about to go to the chapel, she was called into the cellar, where the sisters and some of the wounded had taken refuge. At once a heavy shock was heard. Every moment there were heavy shocks. Our chapel had been struck by a bomb, which destroyed the iron frame of the window, seriously damaged the wall and mouldings, shattered the pews and chairs, and filled all the adjoining rooms with lime and dust. We thought that our whole convent stood in fire and flame. All the window panes in the chapel were out. All the window panes in the front gable of the convent were out. Reverend Mother, who had just escaped death by joining the others in the cellar, returned to her charge in Aertselaar. We four remained in the convent. The doctors assured us that if need be an automobile would be at our disposal in the evening.

Monday, October 5, the chaplain, sent by the major, came to tell us that we must leave. "Go," said he, "not to Antwerp, but through Flanders to England." We thought that our other sisters had already gone to England. We remained Tuesday also, amid the thundering roar of the cannon. At six o'clock in the evening it was announced that the motorcar was ready. "Rapidly," said they. "Everyone away." There we were! One in the kitchen and the others here and there at work. In haste we collected a few of our things, and, without food or other supplies, started on the way to Boom. The Belgian soldiers caused the bridge to spring just when we had crossed it. The two ladies of the Red Cross who had so faithfully assisted in the care of the wounded, were with us. We went from Boom to Hemischen, over a rudely constructed bridge. From this place we jolted and pitched all night long. One of our number, utterly exhausted, slept soundly, and for the time being at least was unconscious of danger or difficulty. At ten o'clock on Wednesday morning we arrived at St. Niklaas.

We were well received by the sisters at the Convent of the Presentation, and remained until next day. Then we went to Ostend. From ten in the morning until five in the evening we remained on the train and spent the night in a convent. We looked for the ambulance, and found it in the "Hotel Splendite," wherein we were given rooms overlooking the sea. There were about three hundred wounded soldiers brought from Antwerp, for that city was just bombarded. We remained there until the 13th of October. We had just retired on the evening of the 13th, when we were hastily called up. *"Toe Zusters' gauw op! Ze zijn hier, alle maal bijna weg."* (Sisters, do hurry up! Nearly all are away from here.) We sprang up, dressed hastily, took our satchels and went directly to the depot.

We stood in the waiting-room from eleven o'clock that night until five next morning. Two trains of wounded soldiers were passing. We succeeded in getting into one of them, and now "Ahead," wherever Divine Providence may lead us. That was a tiresome ride. Every few minutes the train would stop. Where were we going? Probably to France. In a town called Zarren we remained standing a long time. The residents brought food and drink for the soldiers and conducted the Sisters to a convent. We could not find sufficient words to praise and thank these good people; and now again, "Ahead to France."

We arrived in France at eleven o'clock in the night. The people were leaning out of their windows in their night-clothes and calling aloud *"Vive la Belgique! Vive les Heros!"* Again, "Ahead to Dixmunde." Here we were placed on a merchant ship, with one thousand wounded soldiers and *ambulanciers* from Antwerp. We knew not where we were going. There was no food. We slept in a small cabin containing four berths, two above and two below. Those best exercised in gymnastics could climb into the upper beds. A few moments later the two younger sisters had flown into their "Doves' Nest." The ship departed, and finally we arrived in Dover, England. We left Dover and went to Southampton, where we arrived safely on Friday morning. Here the wounded soldiers were taken to hospitals in the city, and we were conveyed to a convent. After a few days we were requested to go to Bristol to teach the Belgian children, and here we are at present among these good English people, where we may possibly remain until the refugees return to Belgium.

A letter from our sisters in Holland last winter states that those members of the community who had taken up their abode in the mission-house of Aertselaar were obliged to leave and take flight a few days later than we. Some of them endured great hardships along the route.

The sisters whom we left in the city wrote about the same time the following:

Our stay in Antwerp was short. We were told that it was dangerous to remain near the Palace of Justice. At six o'clock two of us started to the Touwstraat (Rope street), so as to be near our other sisters. As the street cars had ceased to run, we had to walk about three miles. The sisters who were in the Convent of the Sacred Heart, in Antwerp, could no longer remain, as those nuns also were preparing to leave. It was impossible to close our eyes during that terrible night on account of the thundering, deafening explosions of cannon, while bullets, shells and shrapnel were flying over the city.

Early in the morning we were ready to leave Antwerp, but our older sisters could not walk, and we had also in our company a sick sister from Londerziel. Finally, about eleven o'clock, we left for the station. We could hardly get through because of the crowd and the great number of wagons. Two of us walked on and arrived in Capellen at three o'clock. At the station we had to get into a wagon which had been used for the transportation of cattle, and then away again. At half-past four we were in Calmpthout We waited in the station from half-past nine until four o'clock. Finally we obtained a place in a coal car and set out for Holland.

In Esschen, near the boundary line, we stepped off and walked forth to Hoogerheide, in Holland, where thirty of us will remain in a convent. I had forgotten to say that four of our sisters took flight from Antwerp at one o'clock in the night.

Here in Holland we are eating rye bread and mashed potatoes, passing the night on straw beds stretched upon the floors, and are quite at our ease, for the present at least.

CHAPTER 16

The Exodus to England

All the sisters who had arrived at Antwerp met in conference several times during the week; but no final course of action could be decided upon, owing to the danger and uncertainty which, like dark, ominous clouds, cast a pall over the city and presaged disaster.

One afternoon two of us called on His Eminence, Cardinal Mercier, Archbishop of Mechelen, who, since the bombardment of his city and the destruction of his residence, had remained at times in rooms near the cathedral of Antwerp. His stately countenance was calm and peaceful, notwithstanding the trials and overwhelming sorrows he had endured. We could hardly control our feelings when the fatherly hand of this good and faithful shepherd was raised to bless us for the journey and undertakings we had in view.

On Saturday, October 10, we met in conference for the last time in the Jesuit rooms in Antwerp. Our sisters had no idea of leaving the city at that time. The last advice of our Reverend Director before leaving was:

Observe well the regulations, be ever true to God and duty, and let no day pass without doing some good work.

He is dead now, having peacefully passed away on the night of December 24, 1914, shortly after returning to his former residence in Willebroeck. Although an invalid for years, he was an example of perfect zeal and accuracy in the performance of every duty. He was noted as an author of hymns and poems, and left many important works on Church and Bible history.

Requiescat in pace (rest in peace).

Having parted with our sisters on the street in front of the church, in company with Miss Broelinckx, I went at once to the docks of Antwerp to make arrangements for crossing over to England. About noon on that day a flag was hoisted on the lofty spire of one of the great churches, denoting "Antwerp in danger." In a short time the whole city was panic-stricken. People carrying large and small bundles were seen hurrying through the streets. At noon the signal was removed and confidence restored. At the docks we found that the last passenger boat was just ready to leave on her final trip and could accommodate no more, being then full to overflowing.

Three different times we returned to the docks, but found no means of departure. Even the small merchant boats were overloaded. Finally, on Monday, October 12, I found a place on a small boat, which seemed fit for sailing on an ordinary creek. There were about sixty or seventy refugees on board. I then bade farewell to the beautiful plains of Belgium, to the sisters and acquaintances in whose company we had passed so many happy and peaceful years; farewell to the convent home, where we had learned the one true way to that perfect peace, which neither the storms of time nor the adverse fortunes of war can destroy; farewell to those dear little pupils who daily attended school, the remembrance of whose cheerful, innocent faces inspirit the days of exile, as does the cool, fresh fountain, the weary, way-worn traveller.

Could this parting be final? No! a thousand times no! We shall meet again when these trials are over. The Belgians are a courageous people. Their country will rise from its grave of ashes; her exiled children will return; her cities will stand up from their ruins and flourish as they have never done before, and when kings and *kaisers* have become a memory, sisters will be found at the bedside of the dying, and in the schools to teach the little children, and offer refuge to virtue and innocence within the convent walls.

We took our places on the deck of this little boat at one o'clock. The deck was not covered in any manner, and there were seats for about half of the number of passengers; but we crowded together as best we could, with a certain feeling of security, for we all knew that within a few hours we would be safely out of reach of those terrible bombs and shrapnel, and we had a firm belief that our friends in Antwerp would also succeed in finding a place of safety.

We had just left the docks bound for Flushing, Holland, when the rain began to fall in torrents and a heavy wind came up. We huddled together under the few umbrellas and tried to have patience with our steamboat and the weather. One young lady, in the act of looking around, had the unspeakable chagrin of seeing her umbrella snatched out of her hand by the wind and carried away down the tide. A large ship at some distance, seeing the strange-looking object on the wave, rapidly approached, lowered a boat, and immediately the umbrella was taken on board.

About three o'clock we were out at sea. There was no land to be seen. The wind grew stronger every moment, and our little boat rose and fell, pitched and rolled, in a most alarming manner. Being on the open deck, in the piercing cold wind, kept most of us from an attack of seasickness. Some of the Belgian women, who had never been at sea before, were nearly frantic with terror, and no wonder, for it was certainly a heavy sea for such a small boat. How delighted we were when the lights of Flushing, like so many stars reflected in the sea, began to gleam in the distance. When we entered the harbour the wind ceased and the waves settled down into a calm, dark, lakey surface.

Unfortunately, we had no opportunity of seeing much of this noted summer resort, as it was quite dark when we left our little boat and stepped into a large, pretty looking Mall boat, which carried passengers to and from England.

After supper in the neatly furnished dining-room, we retired to our cabin. We considered ourselves at a safe distance from the firing line, and anticipated a good night's rest. In this we were sadly disappointed. Scarcely had we closed our cabin door, when the ship's crew began to load the boat with her cargo, and the unendurable noise continued all night long. One old lady, who had suffered greatly in coming over from Antwerp, began to scold at everybody and everything, then laughed heartily, turned over in her berth and tried to rest.

Morning dawned, at last. The rain had ceased and the sun was shining brightly. We expected a pleasant voyage over to Folkestone, England. Again we were disappointed. Fearing the mines which might have been encountered on the usual course, our boat had to take another route. Instead of a pleasant trip of three or four hours, we had a voyage of nine hours. On this occasion there was no chance to escape the seasickness. The sea was rougher here than in some places on the Atlantic ocean. Heavy waves dashed against our little boat and caused her to roll and pitch terribly, while a cold, penetrating wind swept the deck like a hurricane.

Some of us became so greatly indisposed that we were advised to go on deck. We did so and stood grasping the railing for an hour or two. Everyone was ill. While on deck we sighted something projecting from the sea, but could not clearly distinguish the outline. It proved to be a submarine; at any rate, we were told that it was; but our boat managed to keep at a safe distance and hastened forth unmolested.

A short time afterward we were signalled by a warship. All action in our boat ceased. The warship drew near and was soon alongside of the Mallboat. An officer came on board to ask if there were soldiers among the passengers. Having received a negative answer, greetings were exchanged and the warship departed, greatly to the satisfaction of all on board. Having lost about half an hour, our steamer forged ahead again at full speed.

About three o'clock, benumbed with cold and indisposed, we staggered to the gangway and were assisted downstairs, where we tried to rest for a time. About five o'clock in the evening the hills and rugged banks of England made their appearance. At six o'clock we entered the harbour of Folkestone. Everyone was obliged to show his or her passport and undergo the doctor's examination. This occupied just an hour. Happy to again set foot on "*terra firma*," we hastened to the train, which stood waiting to take us to London, a ride of two or three hours. In the meantime darkness had closed in and we saw nothing outside of our compartment until after nine o'clock, as we approached the suburbs of London.

CHAPTER 17

London and Leeds

One of the first things to attract attention, as we approached the city, was the double-decked street car. It was so strange to see the people sitting in those box-like cases, up on top of the car. From appearances, one would think this kind of conveyance in danger of tipping over at every turn of the street

A little before ten o'clock we steamed into Victoria Station, London, and immediately made our way to the office of the Relief Committee, who kindly exchanged our Belgian money for English currency and gave us cards to the Premier Hotel, Southampton Row, Russel Square, London.

The Belgians who came to England on this occasion were people of the wealthier class, who paid their own expenses and were free to take rooms or lodgings where they desired; while a great many others who came over at the expense of the Relief Committee were obliged to accept what was assigned them and remain where they were sent until transferred by the Relief Committee.

When all of us met at table in the Premier Hotel, it was quite difficult for the Belgians to make themselves understood. Fortunately, one of the party, being familiar with the two languages, acted as interpreter until each obtained what he or she desired, and the regulations and requirements had been explained.

At half-past eleven all retired to their rooms for the night with feelings of heartfelt gratitude to the good God, who led our steps through so many trials and dangers to a place of peace and safety.

In the morning the whole party attended Mass at eight o'clock in a large church on Southampton Row, and returned to the hotel for breakfast at half-past nine. In the dining hall we met another party of Belgians, among whom were Sister M. Aloise and her family, Mr. and

Miss Erix, of Willebroeck, and the *burgomaster* of Mechelen (Malines) and his wife. The sisters, not having seen each other in several weeks, had a long and pleasant visit After dinner we called on the American Relief Committee and obtained the loan of money necessary for the trip to America. The American Government had made arrangements with its committee to assist in this way American citizens stranded in the belligerent countries. It was given in exchange for a note for the required sum, payable on demand to the United States Treasury after the first of January, 1915. Interest on this note was not exacted.

This action on the part of the American Government, in assisting her stranded citizens who found themselves unable to secure funds at a time when it was impossible to communicate with or receive assistance from friends, was highly praised by prominent Europeans, and deeply appreciated by the Americans themselves.

The important places which we had an opportunity of seeing during this short stay in London were the Tower of London, so noted in English history, the Houses of Parliament, Westminster Abbey, and also the beautiful new Westminster Cathedral, which seems to resemble Westminster Abbey in its mode of construction.

While at the station I sent a dispatch to relatives in Leeds to meet me there at the depot next day, after which we returned to the Premier Hotel for another night. This night, October 15, seemed very long, as I was anxious to proceed on my journey as rapidly as possible. Next morning found the city enwrapped in a heavy "London fog." The streets were very dusty, the air chilly, and the mist so dense that it was impossible to read the names on the buildings across the way.

The streets and thoroughfares of London were so crowded at times that it seemed impossible to pass through. Teams, carriages, street cars, motorcars and pedestrians thronged hither and thither, each with some particular aim or object in view.

Not a single thought of death seemed to occupy their minds, although death could have befallen hundreds of them at every turn of the street. All were in a hurry, for, as a rule, people do not walk in England, they run, which, by the way, impressed me as unusual, considering the fact that the country appears to be very hilly and many of the streets run up or down high hills.

Policemen stand in the middle of the streets at the crossings and keep back the crowds on one side until they have passed on the other.

On all sides placards were posted on the gates and walls calling for

192

recruits to the army. Whole companies of these were seen in citizens' dress marching away to the barracks.

During a very short but pleasant stay in England our attention was often attracted by the zeal of the English woman, working for their absent countrymen. Every spare moment was employed for this purpose. On the train, in the street car, or walking along the streets, her deft fingers were ever busy knitting for some poor soldier at the front

The prayers of thousands of those poor victims freezing in the trenches during the past two winters will call down blessings upon these busy workers, not only in England, but in our own dear country also; and all over the world where this charitable work is undertaken.

On Thursday evening, October 15, I took leave of our numerous Belgian companions and departed alone on the long and tedious journey to Leeds, where I arrived at the appointed hour and was met at the station by relatives, with whom I started at once for their residence.

We enjoyed two or three days of pleasant weather in this busy manufacturing city, and visited some of the churches and places of special interest. The busiest place in the city was, probably the American penny store. Here it was that the Star-spangled Banner gladdened the heart of any American who happened to pass that way and stop for a penny's purchase. Except on Sunday, this immense building was said to be crowded every day in the week, and on Saturdays it was hardly possible to pass through because of the throngs of people who filled it from morning till evening.

One remarkable feature about the city of Leeds is the deep dark colour of the exterior of nearly all the buildings. The cathedral, the City Hall, the museum, and even the statue of Queen Victoria, on the square in front of the City Hall, are of such a dark colour that one would suppose them to be built of black stone. This is probably caused by the fogs, and smoke from the numerous factories. The fog becomes so dense in the fall and winter that the street cars are said to collide, and other accidents occur at times owing to the impossibility of distinguishing objects even at a short distance. When but a few days in Leeds, my attention was attracted by an article in the morning paper announcing the expected arrival of five hundred Belgian refugees in the city.

CHAPTER 18

The Refugees in England

As a good and loving mother would receive her own weary, way-worn children, so did England and Holland open their arms to receive, console, assist and provide for the destitute, war-chased people of Belgium. These unfortunate refugees, the homeless and penniless exiles from a once free and happy country, have been welcomed to the shores of England with a true Christian charity and hospitality, which excites our admiration.

The gates of her manors, the doors of her castles, the dwellings of her citizens, have opened wide to harbour the throngs of refugees who entered her seaports in search of food and shelter. Great numbers went to London and were received in the Alexandria Palace, where on one occasion about three thousand were said to have attended the Divine sacrifice of the Mass and were addressed in their own language by the Rt Rev. Bishop Dewachter, Vic. Gen. to His Eminence Card. Mercier. of the Archdiocese of Mechelen. In this palace they were received and cared for temporarily. Later they were distributed in groups to the different towns and cities of the country in accordance with the means of accommodation afforded by the respective places.

Belgian Relief Committees were established in all the localities about to receive refugees. These, were made up of a number of ladies and gentlemen, both Catholic and Protestant, of the wealthier class of English society. The lord mayor of the city, arid mayors of the towns and villages, took the work of these committees under their special supervision. They were present at the arrival of the refugees and delivered addresses of welcome. The lady mayoress, by her presence and example, often assisted and encouraged the ladies in the clothing department, and when time permitted drove around to visit the Belgians in their new homes. All the ladies and gentlemen of the relief committees were regarded as honorary members and received no compensation for their services.

It is impossible to describe the amount of care, labour and anxiety, not to speak of the time and expense, which these good people encountered in this new field of labour. "I have not had two hours' rest any night since the work began," said Alderman C——, a member of the Bradford Committee, a few days before our departure. The same remark could well have been made by all the members, who devoted their whole time and energies to the work in hand.

The relief committees were obliged to make arrangements for the reception and temporary lodgings of the refugees; also for their wearing apparel and food supplies, because many of them had left their homes with the same clothing which they wore at their ordinary work, and had no other garments with them. Arrangements had to be made with the vicars, or ministers of the Protestant parishes, and with the lords of the manors and castles, as to the permanent dwellings and food supplies of these people during their stay in England; and, to avoid confusion, all had to be in readiness upon the arrival of the refugees, who were sent in large numbers from Alexandria Palace, London. In less than three weeks over fifteen hundred had been received in Leeds, Bradford and Keighley.

When a party of refugees was expected, the whole city, it may be said, turned out to welcome them. The streets from the station to the City Hall, where they usually lodged for a few days, were thronged with curious spectators, long before the appointed hour. They not only filled the streets, but climbed upon every available vantage point in order to see the Belgians. Some little boys had found a place on the pedestal of the statue of Queen Victoria and sat there quite contentedly. Lines of motor cars stood waiting at the station, while the police had great difficulty in keeping back the crowds, who threatened to crush each other in their eager desire to get near the platform.

The first party, over five hundred in number, which was received in Leeds, was expected one evening at five o'clock. Being detained in London, they did not arrive until about twelve o'clock, and yet that immense multitude remained waiting on the street. The danger and inconvenience which await strangers, unaccustomed to the habits and language of a foreign country was anticipated, precautions being taken by the lord mayor and Relief Committee for the purpose of protecting these people, who were regarded as the guests of the nation. Two armed policemen kept unbroken watch at the entrance to the reception hall, and no one was permitted to enter who was not in some manner connected with the work of the Relief Committee. They were required to have cards of admission themselves. Though not obliged to do so, all those connected with this work wore the Belgian colours.

Two Little Sisters of the Poor of England and a sister from Belgium, who acted as interpreter, were requested to remain on guard in the woman's department during the night, while a policeman performed the same duty in the men's part of the building.

When the refugees reached the station, they were received by members of the Relief Committee, and while the cheers and greetings of the assembled multitudes resounded on all sides, they were taken in motor cars to the City Hall or other public building, where a bounteous supper awaited them. Food was abundant. There was soup and meat; bread, butter, fruit and preserves, with plenty of coffee, and boiled milk for the little children. How the refugees did enjoy this good meal, the first which many of them had tasted since they left their own homes in Belgium.

An address of welcome was then delivered by the lord mayor of the city, which was translated into the Flemish language, and responded to by one of the several Belgian priests who were resident pastors in England, and who met the refugees at the station, or came to the City Hall for this purpose.

After supper, all retired as quickly and quietly as possible. A sufficient number of mattresses, sheets, blankets, pillows and shawls had been provided by the wealthy residents. The mattresses were stretched out upon the floors of several large rooms, about a foot apart, and there the beds made up. A separate room was arranged for mothers with small children. Some of these little ones were so ill and tired that they cried all night long.

One child was only seventeen days old. He was born in Alexandria Palace, and, being the first Belgian born on English soil, received the name of Albert George Alexander, and the gift of a beautiful silver watch from an English princess, with his royal name engraved upon it. One poor woman told of having kept her child, three months old, from starving by giving it sugar with water from the ditches along the route. Truly no distinction was here to be observed between rich or poor, high or low class of people. All were grateful to receive the lowly place of rest offered on the floors of the museum, with the costly paintings on the walls around them. A poor old woman was suffering from asthma and was taken to the Home of the Little Sisters of the Poor, where in a few days she was found to be in a dying condition.

Next morning we took some food to a gentleman about eighty-five years old, who, with his wife and adopted daughter, had fled from St. Rombout's Cathedral during the bombardment of the city of Mechelen. He had been the proprietor of a large iron foundry in that city, and in his business had amassed a considerable fortune. As his health began to decline, he sold the foundry and bought fifteen houses to rent. Because of the unexpected attack on the city he was obliged, with many others, to take flight, not having had time to return home for money, clothing or even a handkerchief. He was very ill with bronchitis, and was also taken to the Little Sisters of the Poor.

Next morning many of the refugees attended Mass in the nearest Catholic Church, after which they returned for breakfast at eight o'clock. The tables were well supplied with bread, butter, coffee, fruit, preserves and crackers, or small cookies. After breakfast discourses were delivered to the assembled Belgians, explaining the customs and habits of the country in which they were about to reside, and instructions and information given. At the close of this address the work of registration, which, in some cases was begun the evening before, was continued. The names and residences, the number of members in each family, the daily occupation of each and other particulars were carefully recorded, special care being taken to keep all the members of families and relatives in groups together.

One thing which occasioned great anxiety to nearly all the refugees was the fact that some member, and in a number of cases several members, of their families was missing. In these cases the relief committees advertised in the newspapers, making public the names and former residences of the missing parties, and thus sought in every manner to obtain information regarding them. In many cases they were successful, greatly to the joy of the refugees.

A woman from the vicinity of Antwerp aroused the special sympathy of all who met her. She, with her husband and several children, in company with other refugees, left Antwerp on a train bound for Holland. Several Belgian soldiers were also on the train. During the journey they were fired upon by the enemy. The engineer sprang from the locomotive and ran away. Many of the refugees rushed out of the compartments and, panic-stricken, sought refuge wherever a place of safety could be found. Almost at the same moment one of the soldiers then on the train, who was himself an engineer, sprang into the locomotive, and the train started again on its way to Holland. This all occurred in a few moments. In the confusion which took place when the train was fired upon, this woman's daughter, aged thirteen, unobserved by her parents, had jumped off the train with the others and was left in Antwerp, while the parents and other children were hurried off to Holland, and from Holland to England, having no opportunity to obtain information regarding their lost child.

While the refugees remain at those ancient homesteads, the proprietors have taken upon themselves the responsibility of providing everything needed in the line of food and clothing, the Belgians being required only to prepare their own food and to do their own work. This situation was somewhat trying for the wealthier class, who were in no way accustomed to ordinary labour. In each locality some one was appointed to take the refugees to the nearest Catholic church until they became familiar with the streets and knew the way themselves.

Through the zeal and generosity of the Lord Mayor and Lady Mayoress of Bradford, and prominent members of the Relief Committee in Leeds and Keighley, who not only gave us the use of their motor cars several times, but also, when not engaged, accompanied those who visited the refugees, we had the satisfaction of calling upon many of the Belgians in their new homes. This courtesy afforded us also a good opportunity of seeing and admiring those stately old castles and the lovely groves and grounds which surround them.

We saw the remains of the old Kirkstall Abbey, there in the valley among the hills of Yorkshire.

On a brass tablet in the chapter house is found the following inscription:

THE CITY OF LEEDS.
Pro Rege et Lege.
Kirkstall Abbey.

This Abbey was founded by Henri de Laci, Baron of Pontefract, in the year 1147. It was first established at Barnoldswick, in Craven, by the Cistercian Order of Monks. In the year 1152 the monks removed from Barnoldswick to Kirkstall, and on the present site erected a temporary church. The present church and claustral buildings were completed during the life of the first abbot, who died in the year 1182.

———

This Abbey was surrendered to the Crown at the Dissolution

of Monasteries, on November 22nd, 1539. The Abbey and part of the adjoining lands were acquired from the representatives of the late

Earl of Cardigan,
Colonel J. T. North,

a native of Leeds, and presented by him to the Corporation of Leeds in the year 1889, during the mayoralty of Alderman John Ward, J. P., to be held in trust for his fellow-citizens as a place of public resort and recreation forever.

The Works of Preservation were completed by the Corporation in the year 1895, during the mayoralty of Alderman Peter Gilston, J. P.

As a skeleton protruding from a grave of the past, so appears the empty frame of this ancient structure. The church-like form of the chapel, where the monks of old chanted the divine Office and said their daily prayers; the old, crumbling belfry, where the doves coo and wild birds make their nests; the altar, the refectory and other apartments within, are yet clearly distinguishable. But the storm winds, howling through the frameless doors and windows, awake the echoes of those voices long hushed beneath the ruined walls, and recall another period of war, when the destroying flames desecrated this hallowed shrine as do now the bombs and shrapnels the institutions of Continental Europe.

This is one of the most noted of those ancient ruins, and arouses the interest and admiration of all tourists who visit this part of England.

On another afternoon we were shown through an old but well-preserved castle of the seventeenth century, whose low ceilings, stretching out over the spacious halls and parlours, heavy black mouldings and ornamentation form a striking contrast to the design, structure and decoration of the present age. The lady proprietress of this handsome manor was to be seen with the white cap and apron of a nurse, walking to and from her castle, in the service of the refugees.

The pretty rural names given these old homesteads, such as Oakwood, Laurel Grove, Ambleside Avenue, Arnos Vale and many others, lend them another charm and give a romantic touch to their beauty.

While the scenes witnessed among the refugees were, for the most part, sad and depressing, nevertheless a little incident occurred which touched the mirthful chord in our poor human nature, and afforded us the rare pleasure of a good hearty laugh.

One afternoon during the last week of our visit in England a message was received from members of the Relief Committee in Bradford, asking for an interpreter to come to the assistance of some refugees at Oakwood, whose affairs had become complicated. Two of us set out immediately and arrived at the office of the Relief Committee to hold a conference on the subject. It was decided to visit Oakwood at once and make a thorough investigation of the case. A party of three or four ladies, led by the Hon, Mr, D——, of the Relief Committee, arrived in a motorcar at the entrance to the lovely manor of Oakwood just as the heavy branches of the ancient oaks had succeeded in closing out the last rays of the setting sun.

Mr. D—— advanced with a firm determination to make short work of the matter and settle the difficulties with one good bang of his big cane. He entered the portal, followed by the ladies, and stood a moment before the beautiful plate-glass doors, through which the light of the hall lamp was reflecting in all the colours of the rainbow on the oak carvings of the outer doors. Not finding the bell, he tapped gently on the door with the top of his cane. Again and again this act was repeated, but no response came, although voices inside were distinctly audible.

Becoming quite impatient, Mr. D—— lifted his cane and struck the door one or two resounding blows, which were calculated to attract the attention of the indifferent people within. A deathly silence ensued for a few moments, and then a chorus of women's voices began to cry out, "Call the police! Call the police! Tis burglars! What do they mean by coming here and breaking down our doors?"

One old lady approached the door and asked: "Who is there, and what do you want? We're frightened almost to death. Is that the way to do, to come and pound on the door in that manner?" By this time Mr. D—— had succeeded in making himself heard, as he answered in a tone of sincere sorrow, "I beg pardon, ladies, I really beg pardon. I meant no harm. I meant no harm at all."

By this time the door was partially opened and three panic-stricken old ladies appeared within, while Mr. D——, with his hat in one hand and the offending cane in the other, was bowing most meekly and making elaborate excuses to the ladies, who, seeing the humble attitude of the supposed burglar, ceased to call for the police and were disposed to answer any reasonable question.

"Will you be kind enough to lead us to the Belgian refugees?"

asked Mr. D——— .

"But," said one of the ladies, "there are no Belgians here. You've made a mistake. The refugees are living in the castle yonder on the next manor."

Thanking these good ladies for the information, and again begging pardon for intrusion, we left the portal with more humble feelings than when we entered and proceeded to the next castle.

The trouble here originated between two parties of Belgians who, on account of language (the one spoke French, the other Flemish) and whose political views were intensely antagonistic while yet in Belgium, were unable to agree. Some slight changes were made by the Relief Committee and all dissension ceased.

Next morning a dense fog enveloped the entire landscape. The damp, chilly atmosphere seemed to penetrate every nook and corner, and on the streets, at a few yards distance, objects were scarcely visible. Some necessary preparations were made for the long-anticipated voyage to America, and then we patiently awaited the rapidly approaching steamer *St. Paul*, on her way to Liverpool.

CHAPTER 19

Homeward Bound

Saturday, October 31, at three o'clock in the afternoon, a mixed assembly met on the pier in Liverpool and gazed, with not a little apprehension, at the roily waters of the harbour and the ever-increasing clouds of mist

The *St. Paul*, while not one of the largest or most pretentious of the American steamers, is by no means the least Nineteen years ago she passed us in mid-ocean, although she had left New York three days later than we. Her parlours, refectory, and even the berths, are exceedingly neat and comfortable. The dining-room is particularly attractive. One thing especially noticeable on this ship is the absence of all disagreeable, smoky or gaseous odours, which on some steamers taint even the best-prepared viands, and often cause a feeling of nausea the moment one enters the gangway.

May her patron, the good St Paul, who on earth had taken so many perilous journeys on land and sea, ever watch over his graceful white sea-bird and lead her safely into the wished-for harbour.

Promptly at five o'clock the gong, sounding through the gangway, gave notice of departure. For an hour or two we stood on deck and gazed out upon the rapidly retreating lights of Liverpool, casting their rays so awkwardly through the heavy fog which decked both land and sea.

When the last light fades out on the shore and despondency overwhelms poor human nature, exposed to the unseen dangers of the deep, then confidence is restored by the thought that we are ever in the presence of Him whose watchful eye never closes, and without Whose knowledge not even a sparrow falls to the ground.

CONFIDENCE

God is on the sea,
As well as on the land
Since all the mighty powers that be
Are resting in His hand.

He who gently moves the deep,
And holds the firmament above,
Will His people safely keep.
Who are trusting in His lore.

He who rules the swelling wave,
When the storm is raging nigh,
Can our tortured spirits save
From His Throne of Grace on high.

And should the angel, Death,
Spread his wings above the wave,
Then our last, our dying breath.
Must be: Save! Oh Jesus, save!

Grant us Thy celestial joy
In the realms of love and light,
Where no toils, no cares annoy.
The just one, in Thy sight.

Bring our spirits home to Thee,
Where the angels' joyous band,
Far above the deep, dark sea,
'Round Thy throne forever stand.

Before concluding, it may not be out of place to refer particularly to the noble feelings of fraternal charity which existed among the English people, not only in regard to the Belgians, whom they so generously received and housed, but also with respect to their conduct toward their Catholic fellow-citizens engaged with them in this charitable work. We heard no more of those petty enmities which so often had arisen in times past as to race, creed or nationality. The Catholic priest and Protestant minister worked side by side in this good work. Ladies of every denomination united their efforts and offered their time and money for the sole purpose of helping the needy. No compensation was expected, no material gains to be obtained. Thus every work performed was a work of perfect self-sacrifice, and deserved a greater reward than earth can repay. A golden link in the chain of love will ever more unite the hearts of England and Belgium.

Further experience has shown that these golden links have multiplied until the chain extends across the Atlantic, and holds in its friendly tangles the heart of America also; who, of her rich abundance, has dealt out to Belgium the clothing and life-giving foodstuffs which during the past two years have saved the country from famine.

When this period of anguish is over and historians are recording for future generations the horrors of this awful conflict, may they also give just praise to the All-wise Being who has caused the fragrant rose of charity to bloom among the weeds of war.

We were, or seemed to be, far out in the Irish Sea before we could tear ourselves away from that wonderful sight. The sea was as yet quite calm, and a number of hungry seagulls were flying around as if to bid us a last farewell; so we remained on deck until it was found necessary to enter and make arrangements for the night.

We were sadly disappointed on that dismal Hallow E'en in not being able to obtain a glimpse of our own dear little Emerald Isle, so near and dear, and yet so far away.

Next morning, Sunday, Feast of All Saints, found us out in the deep waters of the channel, but the sea still remained calm. At half-past seven o'clock we assisted at the Holy Sacrifice of the Mass, offered up in one of the ship's parlours.

When the service was ended we returned to our rooms, where in a few hours we were all undergoing severe attacks of seasickness.

When again we walked the deck it was to inhale the invigorating salt sea breeze and admire the wondrous waste of waters with the clear blue sky above, and in the depths reflected a most beautiful picture, "Sunset on the Sea."

A day or two later we encountered on board, a Belgian woman *en route* for Illinois, where her daughter was living. She had only sufficient money to pay her passage to New York City, and, being unable to speak the English language, was in great distress. The necessary sum was donated by a Catholic clergyman of Massachusetts, by a Belgian gentleman who was on board, and a lady of the "Committee for the Protection of Travellers." All needful information was given, and when we arrived in New York City she was safely placed on the midnight train for Illinois.

Thus ended a short but fascinating mission among the Belgian refugees in England. Thus ended the troubles, trials and sorrows of three months in "The Great War."

May the gory cloud soon disappear from the eastern skies and nev-er, never darken the gold and azure of our own American horizon.

www.ingramcontent.com/pod-product-compliance
Lightning Source LLC
Chambersburg PA
CBHW032057080426
42733CB00006B/312